The Business Sale...
An Owner's Most
Perilous Expedition

Guiding Techniques
From Merger &
Acquisition
Professionals

Written by

Mark Jordan

Mark Gould

Rick Dillon

Jeffrey Presogna

David L. Perkins, Jr.

Compiled and Published by VERCOR
5590 Bunky Way, Atlanta, GA 30338
Voice Toll Free: 877-274-7323, Fax: 770-399-5883
Email: info@vercoradvisor.com
www.vercoradvisor.com

Co-Published by The Business Owner, LLC
7010 S. Yale Avenue, Suite 120
Tulsa, OK 74136
Voice: 918-298-9399, Fax: 918-298-0595
www.thebusinessowner.com

Copyright © 2001 by VERCOR

No part of this book may be reproduced or transmitted in any form or by any means, electronic or mechanical, including photocopying, recording, or by any information storage and retrieval system, without permission in writing from the publisher.

About the Authors

The Business Sale...An Owners Most Perilous Expedition is a collaborative effort by five mergers and acquisitions advisors: Mark Jordan, Mark Gould, Rick Dillon, Jeffrey Presogna, and David Perkins.

Mark Jordan has a unique, multi-disciplined background comprised of advanced tax strategies, estate, and financial markets knowledge. He also holds a MBA, BS in Business Administration, and various professional designations. He has been involved in numerous transactions both personally and as an advisor. He is currently the President of Capital Strategies, Inc., a middle market mergers and acquisitions firm. He is also founder and managing partner of VERCOR, a middle market mergers and acquisitions firm catering to national accounts.

Mark Gould has owned numerous companies, including medical distribution, printing, manufacturing, and various food related businesses. He holds the designations of Certified Business Intermediary and Certified Business Appraiser. He is president of Gould Business Group and partner of VERCOR.

Rick Dillon has owned several distribution and manufacturing companies. He is president of Dillon-Schramm, a middle market mergers and acquisitions firm, and partner of VERCOR.

Jeffrey Presogna is a CPA and holds a BS in Accounting. In addition to his unique tax background, he holds the designation of Certified Valuation Analyst. He is president of Presogna and Associates and partner of VERCOR.

David L. Perkins, Jr. holds a BA in psychology and MBA with a concentration in accounting. He is also a Certified Business Intermediary, real estate broker, and is licensed to sell insurance. He is president of Acquisition Advisors; Chief Executive Office of The Business Owner, LLC; and is a shareholder in a money-management firm and real estate development company.

Warning - Disclaimer

The area of mergers and acquisitions is a very complex field and encompasses many disciplines. This book is designed to be an overview of the process, thereby enabling the reader to gain a greater understanding of the process.

This book is sold with the understanding that neither publisher nor authors are engaged in rendering legal, accounting, investment, or other professional advice. If any of these services are required, the reader should seek competent professional assistance.

The reader is encouraged to review all available resources before making a decision regarding the divestiture of his or her business. This book is not the final source or guide and may contain mistakes, both typographical and in content. In addition, much of the information discussed in this book changes as laws change.

Neither the publisher nor authors shall have any liability or responsibility to any person or entity with respect to any loss or damage caused, or alleged to have been caused, directly or indirectly, by the information contained in this book.

If you do not wish to be bound by the above, you may return this book to the publisher for a full refund.

Introduction

Business owners frequently invest many years of time and effort in developing a successful company. Throughout the process, owners make great sacrifices and involve many others who contribute to the business growth over the years. However, factors such as retirement, lack of capital, management gaps, changing industry factors, or a desire for greater liquidity eventually force the business owner to consider selling the company. The old adage "all good things must come to an end" frequently leaves the owner wondering what's next.

Should I sell my company now? Would I get more money if I waited? Who is the right buyer? A business owner must make many important decisions regarding the sale of his or her business and the appropriate timing.

The focus of this book is not on when you should sell or whether or not you should sell. This book is dedicated to providing insight on the mergers and acquisitions process once you have made the determination to divest your business.

After deciding to sell your company, you will begin an expedition that could take as little as a few months or up to several years. Regardless of the timing, it is important to understand the five primary stages in every business transaction:

1. Hiring the Right Intermediary
2. Pre-Sale Planning
3. Marketing
4. Negotiation
5. Closing

The goal of this book is to give owners a greater understanding of the process and the ingredients that go into a successful business sale. A chef does not become a master at his trade because he knows a few of the ingredients to a great recipe. Likewise, a business owner typically cannot manage this process as well as an intermediary who has all of the ingredients and has been "preparing the dish" for many years.

Each stage of the process has its own unique set of factors, so this book is divided into the five stages of a business sale process. Each section will provide a highlight of the key steps involved in yielding an effective outcome in the divestiture of a business. When you are finished, you will have a greater understanding of how an intermediary guides a business owner through the often uncharted terrain of selling a company.

Contents

About the Authors   iii
Disclaimer   iv
Introduction   v

Section I
Hiring The Right Intermediary

Chapter 1. Key Benefits of Using an Intermediary	3
Chapter 2. What to Look for in an Intermediary	15
Chapter 3. The Engagement Agreement	23

Section II
Pre-Sale Planning

Chapter 4. Need Analysis	37
Chapter 5. Determining Business Value	47
Chapter 6. Tax Planning and Offering Documents	55
Chapter 7. Recasting Income Statements and Balance Sheets	65

Section III
Marketing

Chapter 8. Buyer Types	73
Chapter 9. Buyer Profiles	79
Chapter 10. Generating Buyer Interest	87
Chapter 11. Retrieving Confidential Documents and Facility Tours	97

Section IV
Negotiation

Chapter 12. Defining the Negotiation Process	105
Chapter 13. Setting the Stage	109
Chapter 14. Developing the Proposal	115
Chapter 15. Debate	121
Chapter 16. Final Negotiation and Agreement	133

Section V
Closing

Chapter 17. Structuring the Transaction	137
Chapter 18. Tax Considerations of Transaction Types	153
Chapter 19. Due Diligence	165
Chapter 20. Closing Documents and Procedures	179

With respect, we dedicate this book to business owners everywhere whose hard work, perseverance, and vision have been the foundation of economies around the world.

Section I

Hiring the Right Intermediary

Chapter 1
Key Benefits of Using an Intermediary

Once a business owner decides to sell a business, he or she needs to determine who will handle the process. There are only two options – manage the process personally or delegate it to a business intermediary. The three chapters in this section are focused on helping you understand the benefits of using an intermediary, what to look for in an intermediary, and what to expect in the terms of an engagement agreement you will eventually sign with an intermediary. Lastly, you will see inserts throughout this section named **"Common Pitfalls"** which illustrate some of the more common mistakes business owners make when managing the process themselves.

To begin illustrating the importance of hiring an intermediary, we will look at a recent encounter with an owner called "Jack". Jack owns a telecommunications company with revenues of $5,000,000. Due to his success in sales, Jack thought he knew how to manage the process of selling his company. Jack's company featured a distinctive asset that was of great interest to several large buyers.

Key Benefits of Using an Intermediary

Jack contacted the buyers directly (without a confidentiality agreement) to inform them of his desire to sell. One of the individuals, which we will call Buyer A, expressed interest and assembled a letter of intent after repeated discussions with the owner. Jack and Buyer A revised the letter of intent over the next several months until both were satisfied.

Meanwhile, another buyer, Buyer B, surfaced with his own letter of intent. Jack decided to try and secure a better deal with Buyer B, so he put Buyer A on hold. Jack spent the next two months working on the new letter of intent with Buyer B. Due to the time delay, Buyer A withdrew his offer. All seemed well because Jack was close to a better contract with Buyer B. When he was ready to finalize the arrangement, Buyer B informed him the deal was off. The story got even more interesting when Jack found out that Buyer A entered into an agreement to acquire Buyer B.

Unable to handle the time demands, Jack took too long to close the transaction. He failed to "strike while the iron was hot." Unfortunately, Jack did not have a happy ending. Jack's particular type of asset no longer demands great interest, and he is unable to sell his business. Before deciding to manage the process yourself, make sure you fully understand the risks.

Unlike the seller above, smart sellers will see the merits of hiring a professional mergers and acquisitions firm to manage the process.

Key Benefits of Using an Intermediary

The key advantages to utilizing an intermediary are best described with the acronym **SUCCESS**:

1. Strategic Fit
2. Understand the Process
3. Create Multiple Options
4. Communication / Negotiation
5. Expectations are Managed
6. Stay Focused on the Business
7. Sustain Momentum

Let's look at each of these benefits in more detail.

1. Strategic Fit means synergy between the purchasing entity and the seller. This could take many forms, but a few examples include product, distribution, geographic, and management synergies. Product synergy occurs when the purchaser and seller have complementary products that, when combined, create greater value. Additionally, distribution synergy happens when the purchaser has products that can be distributed through the seller's customer base. Another type of strategic fit is geographic synergy. This is when a purchaser needs a new geographic presence where the seller is currently located. Finally, management synergy occurs when management gaps can be closed upon the purchase of a new company. By striving towards a strategic fit, the business sale yields greater value.

A skilled and experienced intermediary is adept at discovering synergy between buyers and sellers.

5

Case in Point: The owner of a technology company decided to sell her business and hired an intermediary. After the first round of marketing, two potential buyers emerged, both within 10% of the initial asking price. Despite the apparent financial compatibility, neither buyer strategically fit with the seller.

The intermediary continued to pursue a strategic buyer and launched a second round of marketing. From this effort, a strategic buyer emerged with complimentary products and tendered an offer that was twice the value of the previous two offers. The deal closed several months later.

Common Pitfall:
Poor Definition of Strategic Marketability: Business owners often lack a definition of exactly what they have to offer, thereby reducing the likelihood of attracting a strategic buyer.

2. Understanding the Process of selling a company is a vital component to a successful divestiture. Despite the success of many companies, most owners do not fully comprehend all aspects of a business sale transaction. Conversely, an intermediary handles several business deals daily, so they are experienced in all aspects of business sale activities. To better define the process, it is important to understand the basic steps of an intermediary transaction.

The following steps illustrate the typical flow of an

Key Benefits of Using an Intermediary

intermediary transaction:

> Step 1: Initial Meeting
> Step 2: Financial Review of Company
> Step 3: Finalization of Closing Agreement
> Step 4: Pre-Sales Planning
> Step 5: Marketing
> Step 6: Negotiation
> Step 7: Finalizing Deal
> Step 8: Closing

Steps 1 and 2, the initial meeting and financial review, are conducted to determine the probability of success and potential fit between the mergers and acquisitions firm and the seller. Step 3 is finalization of the closing agreement between the intermediary and the seller. Chapter 3 will discuss some of the key terms of such an agreement. The real process of marketing a company begins with Step 4, pre-sales planning, and concludes with Step 8, closing.

Pre-sales planning is a vital part of preparing an organized and comprehensive plan to bring a business to market. It involves extensive company fact finding and industry research. The objective of this step is to complete a "deal book" which outlines key information regarding the company. Section 2 will cover this in depth.

Marketing a business requires a tremendous amount of time and resources while utilizing many different avenues, including industry contacts, deal databases, and

7

marketing outreach. The marketing process and information exchange is discussed in Section 3.

Negotiating involves managing all of the relationships in a transaction and having a keen understanding of each party's goals and objectives. There is no magic formula to succeed in this area, but there is a process that needs to be followed and pitfalls to be avoided. These are discussed at length in Section 4.

The final step is closing the deal. Frequently, the most difficult step is moving all of the interested parties to a successful closing. Even in the best of circumstances this is a complicated process. In Section 5, we share with you some of the nuances of this very important ingredient.

The process of taking a company to market and moving it to closing is very complicated and time consuming. Very few business owners understand the process well enough to manage all facets, and most owners rarely have the time or objectivity. However, a business intermediary experiences all aspects of the process on a regular basis. Unlike a business owner who may have only sold a company one or two times, a business intermediary handles business sale planning, marketing, negotiation, and closing activities on a daily basis.

Common Pitfalls

Incorrect use of non-disclosure agreements and poor screening of prospective purchasers: Most business owners are uncomfortable asking for a non-disclosure agreement or they wait too late to secure one. In

addition, they frequently utilize poor screening methods for buyer candidates.

3. Creating Multiple Options relates to the ability to orchestrate and manage several buyers at the same time. The classic mistake a business owner makes when selling his business is dealing with one interested party at a time. This not only limits an owner's likelihood of landing a successful deal, it also limits the number of potential offers.

To further illustrate the point, here is a common scenario: A potential buyer contacts a business owner expressing an interest in his company. The owner responds by saying "sure, I would consider selling if the price is right." The owner sends information to the buyer (frequently without an effective confidentiality agreement). In the meantime, the buyer is doing nothing to generate additional interest from other prospective buyers. If and when the buyer finally makes an offer, the owner has no idea if he is receiving a strong value because he frequently has no other offers for comparison.

If the marketing outreach process is managed effectively, there is a greater probability of securing several interested parties on each deal. Multiple interested parties means greater clarity in evaluating the merits of each offer, and increases the likelihood that a strong value will be received.

4. Communication and Negotiation is the foundation of every deal, but contrary to popular belief, it is not the only step that matters. This is by far the most

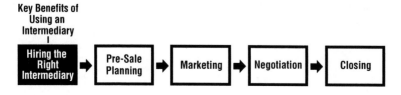

common stumbling block to most business owners. They perceive themselves to be excellent negotiators; therefore they assume they can negotiate the best possible deal. Many times owners forget that a lot more goes into "getting a good deal" than their ability to communicate.

Consider the owner who focuses exclusively on price in his negotiations. He may very well get his price, not realizing the purchaser gladly agreed to it because the structure of the deal heavily favored the buyer. Another common development is "sowing seeds of discord." In an attempt to negotiate the best position, the purchaser or seller unintentionally insults the other, thereby creating an antagonistic relationship. Unfortunately, this conflict sticks with them throughout the process. Therefore, their ability to resolve minor disagreements is greatly impeded.

A professional intermediary is able to "remain above the fray" and eliminate personal feelings. This increases the chance of resolving disagreements and landing a successful deal for both the buyer and seller.

Common Pitfalls

Disclosing an asking price too soon: Business owners often disclose their asking price too early in the process, thereby eliminating the possibility of securing a value beyond their desire.

5. Few sellers know what is reasonable to expect and how to **Manage Expectations**. Is it reasonable to ask for a confidentiality agreement before releasing any information? How much information should I release initially? When

should I meet with the buyer? When should I expect a letter of intent? What about earnest money – how much and when? Who drafts the purchase agreement? When do I tell my employees? How long should I allow for due diligence? Who pays for due diligence? These are just a few of the questions that come up during the process. Knowing what is reasonable dictates how you respond to the buyer and demonstrates your skill level. Small things such as this dictate who controls the process, who bargains from a position of strength, and who gets the better deal.

Many buyers will "tilt the table" to their advantage if they feel a seller is uninformed. The most common approach a buyer uses is "this is the way we always do it." Since the seller has no idea what is reasonable, he naturally assumes the buyer's request must be reasonable. For example, buyers frequently tell a seller they will not provide a letter of interest or value assessment before visiting the seller's facility. When a seller consistently concedes this point to buyers, they end up investing a lot of time with "tire kickers" who are not serious candidates.

Conversely, a mergers and acquisitions professional knows what to expect, how to communicate, and how to deal with any surprise that surfaces during the process.

Common Pitfalls

Loss of control: Business owners lose control of the process and become a responder to the buyer who ends up dictating their every move.

6. The biggest risk a business owner faces when

attempting to manage the process himself is the inability to **Stay Focused on the Business** during the sales process. The owner typically becomes distracted in two ways – time and mental energy. Given the time consuming nature of the process, it is easy for an owner to wake up one day and find he is spending the majority of his time on the transaction. In addition, when managing the process himself, the owner frequently becomes mentally drained. Both of these create a scenario where the business suffers during a critical time.

Consider the following scenario. A business owner has experienced consistent growth over the past three years and decides to sell his company. He spends a significant amount of time contacting prospective buyers and receives numerous inquiries. One interested party comes in for a plant visit and is very impressed. The prospective buyer assembles an additional list of items they would like to review. At this point, the seller has invested several months of time in the process. A problem surfaces when he realizes one of his key accounts has decided to take their business elsewhere. He discovers that the account had been having problems getting proper service, but he was unaware of the problem due to his lack of focus on the business. The lack of focus not only hurts the productivity of the business, but also potentially diminishes his company's value at the most critical time.

A business intermediary is able to manage the sale process while allowing the seller to continue to

focus on running his or her business. The intermediary maintains contact with the owner, but handles the daily business sale efforts so the owner can stay focused on business and maintain marketability.

7. The sale of a business is like any other process – **Sustaining Momentum** is critical. When you have positive momentum during the process, good things tend to happen. Conversely, negative momentum tends to feed on itself.

The typical business owner runs into the following scenario quite often. He begins the process of selling his business, or worse yet, he responds to an inquiry. He invests considerable time in responding to information requests and the buyer begins to exhibit serious interest. The owner then becomes distracted with more pressing issues within his business, such as employee, customer, vendor, or financial problems. As his focus shifts back to his business, he begins to lose momentum with his prospective buyer. The buyer becomes frustrated with a lack of responsiveness and moves on to another deal. The owner must then start the process over again.

By delegating the process to an intermediary, the owner is able to focus on the business, enabling him to be insulated from the ups and downs of the process. Momentum is sustained and prospective buyers are dealt with on a timely basis. Of course, even when an intermediary handles the process, there are no guarantees the deal will close. However, it will not be lost due to a lack of responsiveness or lack of focus on the deal at hand.

Key Benefits of Using an Intermediary

Knowledge is power, especially when deciding to sell a business. For most owners, the business sale process is a mountain of uncertainty. As previously shown, the right advisor is critical for maximizing the selling price of your company. So how do you evaluate advisors and select the right one? The next chapter will help you learn what to look for in an intermediary and how to pick the best advisor to manage the sale of your company.

Chapter 2
What to Look for in an Intermediary

Intermediaries can take on many different forms, but generally there are three broad classes of professional advisors – main street (referred to as business brokers), middle market, and large transaction. Certainly there is overlap among all three classes, but firms tend to fall into one of these three groups. The primary differences between the groups revolve around deal size, methodology, type of buyer, and compensation.

Deal Size refers to the value of the transaction. Main street intermediaries typically focus on transactions with value under $1,000,000. Middle market firms generally focus on transaction values of $1,000,000 to $30,000,000, while large transaction firms handle transactions over $30,000,000.

Methodology relates to the process and systems employed by the intermediary. Main street firms employ a process more akin to real estate sales. They focus on acquiring a large inventory of listings, rely on "business opportunity" advertising, and share deals with other main street brokerage firms. Additionally, main street firms tend to focus on local and community-based businesses, such as restaurants, dry cleaners, pet stores, auto body shops, lawn care, and convenience stores.

Relative to the other segments, they spend a small amount of time on pre-sales planning and packaging. Their informal marketing is primarily local mass advertising and contacts within their personal network.

The middle market mergers and acquisitions firm is characterized by heavy pre-sales planning and proactive marketing outreach. They spend significant time on the front end developing a comprehensive "deal book" that outlines and discusses all of the key components of the sellers business. Their methodology is heavily focused on researching the marketplace to identify strategic buyers and executing a comprehensive marketing campaign to attract their interest. In addition, middle market firms typically maintain an extensive database of financial buyers.

Large transaction firms tend to employ a financial engineering methodology. They spend the greatest amount of time on pre-sales planning and deal structure. The universe of purchasers for large companies is much smaller, so less time is spent on actual marketing. Frequently, the ability to create financial synergy is the motivating factor behind large deals.

The **Type of Buyer** involved in a main street transaction is typically an individual characterized by the following: they are usually looking to buy "a job", they have minimal cash flow, are reliant on seller financing, and have minimal experience as a business owner. In middle market and large transactions, buyers tend to be wealthy businessmen, large privately owned companies, private equity firms, or public companies. They normally have cash available for transactions or have bank financing in place as

well as experience in business acquisitions.

The **Compensation** structure for a main street firm is usually 10% - 15% of the transaction, paid at closing. Middle market and large transaction firms are typically paid in the form of a retainer that is credited against a performance fee. Retainers can range from $10,000 to $50,000 for middle market deals and can reach the $100,000+ range for large transactions. Performance fees can start as high as 10% on the first $1,000,000 in value and decline on each subsequent $1,000,000 in value to 1%.

***Example of Middle Market Fee Structure*:** Based on an $8,000,000 transaction, if a firm charged a $24,000 retainer fee and a performance fee of 7% of the first million, 6% of the second million, 5% of the third million, 4% of the fourth million, 3% of the fifth million, 2% of the sixth million, and 1% of everything over $6 million, the fee would be calculated as follows:

```
Performance Fee Calculation
0$            - $1,000,000 = $70,000
$1,000,001 - $2,000,000 = $60,000
$2,000,001 - $3,000,000 = $50,000
$3,000,001 - $4,000,000 = $40,000
$4,000,001 - $5,000,000 = $30,000
$5,000,001 - $6,000,000 = $20,000
$6,000,001 - $7,000,000 = $10,000
$7,000,001 - $8,000,000 = $10,000
Total Performance Fee   = $290,000
   Retainer Fee Credit  = ($24,000)
Net Due to Intermediary = $266,000 or 3.4%
```

As with any industry, there are both quality firms and inferior firms. Main street, middle market, and large transaction firms each have there own strengths and unique positions in the marketplace. The question is not which type of firm is better, but which one is best suited for your specific deal.

Common Pitfalls
Hiring an intermediary from the wrong segment: Too often sellers don't consider the market specialization of the intermediary they are hiring.

After determining which type of firm has the best fit with your deal, you can turn to the selection criteria for help in choosing a specific intermediary. There are a number of factors you should evaluate when choosing who is going to represent you in the sale of your business. The remaining information of this chapter will focus on six of these factors denoted by the acronym **WEALTH**:

    1. **W**ide Range of Clients
    2. **E**xperience as an Owner
    3. **A**cademics and Credentials
    4. **L**istens to Your Goals
    5. **T**rust and Confidentiality
    6. **H**igh Quality Engagements

1. A **Wide Range of Clients** relates to the intermediary's experience in working on deals that span many different industries. While there can be some

benefit to an intermediary who exclusively focuses on a specific niche, generally speaking, you are better off working with a firm that has dealt with clients in diverse types of businesses. The more industries to which the intermediary has experience, the more buyer contacts he will have.

2. It is also extremely beneficial to find an intermediary who has **Experience as an Owner**. An intermediary who has bought and sold businesses for his personal portfolio has a much greater empathy for the seller. In addition, he has a better understanding for the practical aspects of selling an ongoing business. This also gives the intermediary greater credibility with the prospective buyers.

3. Additionally, an intermediary who has furthered himself through **Academics or Credentials** demonstrates a commitment to professionalism. Certainly, there are exceptions to this guideline. Many in the mergers and acquisitions field have great skills while lacking in the areas of academics and credentials. However, certain professional credentials and specialties, such as advanced tax training, estate and financial markets knowledge, asset/equity transfer and accounting certifications, commonly contribute favorably to the skill-set of the intermediary.

4. More importantly, it is critical to find a professional who **Listens to Your Goals.** Every deal is

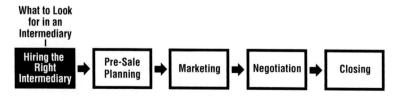

different and every business owner has unique objectives. Especially during the pre-sales planning phase, an intermediary needs to focus on your desires as opposed to a pre-determined plan.

Common Pitfalls
Hiring an intermediary who focuses on their goals instead of yours: There is more to a transaction than "closing the deal." There are many intangibles that need to be considered based on the seller's objectives.

5. Trust and Confidentiality is the single most important factor you should look for in an intermediary who will represent you in the sale of your business. The majority of the time you will not want anyone to know you are contemplating a divestiture. At the very least, you want to have control over who is aware of your plan. The firm you select must have tight control over how information is released to prospective buyers. This starts with an intermediary that does not "talk" and a strict confidentiality agreement that must be signed by every prospective purchaser before they receive substantive information.

6. The last characteristic you should look for is a firm that focuses on **High Quality Engagements**. In other words, you do not want to work with an intermediary who will take any deal that comes along. A firm dedicated to high quality deals will only accept your project if they feel there is a reasonable probability the deal will close. This reduces the risk of wasting your time by embarking

on a project that in all likelihood will not happen.

Of course, even when your selected mergers and acquisitions firm meets all of the criteria and the fit is perfect, there are still no assurances the deal will happen. Naturally, by spending time evaluating your options and making the best choice for you, your opportunity for success is increased.

Once you have selected the best intermediary for your transaction, it is important for you to understand what to expect in an agreement. By educating yourself on the overall factors that should be involved in a contract, you will be better prepared to make the best decision possible for the sale of your company.

Chapter 3
The Engagement Agreement

Due to the personalized nature of each business sale project, most merger and acquisition experts do not follow a standardized agreement format. Depending on the complexity of the transaction, the list of actual details in a contract can be exhaustive. This chapter does not detail a comprehensive list, but it will showcase some of the key points found in most agreements.

Regardless of the format your intermediary uses, you need to make sure the following items, denoted by the acronym **AGREED**, are included:

1. **A**ctual Length of Agreement
2. **G**roup of Services Provided
3. **R**emuneration
4. **E**xpenses
5. **E**xclusivity
6. **D**isclosure

1. The **Actual Length of the Agreement** has two parts: the initial term and the survival period.

Following is a sample of a clause found in an actual engagement agreement:

> "This agreement shall continue in effect for an initial term of twelve calendar months or until Clients' goals are reached, whichever occurs first. This agreement may be extended at any time provided both parties mutually agree. Clients' obligation under this agreement to Intermediary arising out of contacts, activity and/or negotiations initiated during the term of this agreement shall survive this agreement for three (3) years."

The initial term states the period of time the intermediary will actively pursue the marketing of a business sale. Once this period expires, both parties can decide to extend the contract or simply let the agreement dissolve. Upon expiration, the intermediary is still protected for a period of time called the survival period. This means that if the business is purchased by a buyer that had contact with the intermediary during the initial period, the intermediary will still receive his full performance fee. This protects the intermediary from a seller delaying the close of a deal to circumvent the performance fee.

Common Pitfalls

Expecting a transaction to occur too quickly: Many business owners expect deals to occur within a few months. As a

result, the owner looks for agreements that are too short in length of time. A talented intermediary will not agree to a term that is insufficient to get a deal done.

2. The next item of importance in an agreement outlines the **Group of Services Provided**. While it is impossible to list every possible activity, there should be an outline covering the main components of the intermediary's service.

Some of the service details include the confidential profile, confidential memorandum, targeted outreach, plant visits, due diligence, formal offers, negotiation, and closing. To illustrate, excerpts from actual intermediary agreements follows:

> *"In concert with Client, Intermediary will formulate and implement an objective based strategy which will include, when necessary, the following steps.*
>
> *Confidential Profile: The development of a confidential profile on Client's company outlining key elements of the business."*

The **Confidential Profile** is also known as an executive summary and provides a brief overview of the business. Generally, it does not disclose the name of the company, but gives enough information for a prospective buyer to determine if the pursuit of additional information is merited.

"Confidential Memorandum: The compilation of a detailed memorandum outlining history, management, marketing, financials, etc."

The **Confidential Memorandum** is also known as a "deal book", "project document", "offering document" or "prospectus". It discloses the name of the company being offered and discusses the key aspects of the business. This is released after the prospective purchaser has signed a confidentiality agreement.

"Targeted Outreach: Intermediary will direct a targeted outreach including mailings, centers of influence, and direct phone contact."

This states what the intermediary will be responsible for within the **Marketing Campaign**. While it is likely that you as the seller will provide some contacts to the intermediary, it is the intermediary's job to oversee and coordinate the marketing effort.

Common Pitfalls

Eliminating prospective buyers before they are ever contacted: Business owners typically have preconceived notions regarding potential buyers. You never know for sure if a buyer is interested until initial contact.

"Plant Visits: Intermediary will assist in coordinating plant visits and

preliminary due diligence."

The **Plant Visit** statement expresses the intent of the intermediary to facilitate all plant visits and coordinate scheduling. Company visits are very time consuming, so it is critical that the intermediary take charge of this activity.

Common Pitfalls
Allowing prospective purchasers to visit your facility too soon: Buyers generally want to visit the facility and meet the owner early in the process – owners acquiesce on this point too often.

Due Diligence deals with the process of providing detailed records to a prospective purchaser after a letter of intent or purchase agreement has been executed. The intermediary will facilitate the process, but there will be significant involvement on the part of the business owner at this juncture.

> "*Formal Offers: Intermediary will coordinate formal offers of price and Letters of Intent.*"
> "*Negotiations: Intermediary will assist to whatever extent necessary in the negotiation process.*"

While the business owner makes the ultimate decision regarding the acceptability of any deal, it is the intermediary's job to **Negotiate** on behalf of the business owner. In addition, the intermediary will receive, review,

and explain all **Offers and Letters of Intent** that are presented.

Common Pitfalls
Painting yourself into a corner: Sellers are often too rigid about what they will and will not do too early in the negotiation process. This leaves little room to concede points later in the process.

> *"Closing: Intermediary will assist in coordinating the arrangements surrounding closing."*

The **Closing** process is an extensive and complicated process. Multiple relationships need to be managed and many conflicts need to be resolved. It is important that your intermediary be the quarterback of this process. Naturally, you will have legal counsel that is responsible for memorializing the agreement and handling closing day, but the intermediary must be the overseer.

Common Pitfalls
Losing control of the closing process: Too often sellers are left out of the loop during the closing process and miss opportunities to address obstacles before they become problems.

Obviously, the above samples do not contain complete language and would not be appropriate to use in

drafting an agreement. The intermediary you select will provide you with an agreement, but make sure the above items are addressed clearly.

3. In chapter 2, we discussed **Remuneration** and the different methods of compensating an intermediary. This is one of the most important details clearly laid out in your agreement.

> *"Retainer: In the event of a successful transaction, a credit will be applied against the success fee detailed below for all retainers paid."*

Note the retainer is not refundable, but is credited against the performance fee if the deal closes.

> *"Success Fee: Intermediary will receive 7% of the first million, 6% of the second million, 5% of the third million, 4% of the fourth million, 3% of the fifth million, 2% of the sixth million, and 1% of everything over $6 million of all consideration received for the businesses."*

Note the success fee or performance fee is paid on all consideration received for the business. The business owner may have choices as to how he accepts the structure of his deal: all cash, seller financing, stock, royalty, etc. However, the intermediary gets his corresponding percentage on all components of the deal.

> "*Consideration: The amount used as consideration in determining Intermediary's compensation from a transfer or change of ownership of share capital or assets of will be the sum of all amounts used by the parties in determination of net settlement. This includes, but is not limited to, such consideration as payments in cash; stock; options; notes or other evidence of indebtedness; assumption of, or relief from debt or liabilities including personal and corporate debt; earn-out (when paid); consulting agreements or covenants not to compete; and all other assets to be exchanged in connection with the transfer of ownership.*"

Typically, you will find an agreement goes into great detail about consideration so there is no misunderstanding among parties. You may choose to receive all of your deal in stock in a public company, but the intermediary will receive his percentage in cash based on the value of the deal at closing.

> "*Payment: The fee, as calculated above, shall be paid in US dollars in full at closing in cash, money order, or by escrow account check.*"

The entire performance fee is paid at closing with one exception – an earnout. An earnout occurs when a business owner receives a percentage of a benchmark (sales, gross profit, etc.) over an extended period of time. For example, one might receive 2% of sales over the next five years. Since this number fluctuates and is not measurable at

closing, the intermediary is typically paid his percentage when you receive payment each year.

4. Additionally, who pays **Expenses** is an important issue to address in any agreement.

> *"Client shall pay airfare, rental car, and hotel, if necessary, which they have approved in advance, for intermediary's travel to any meeting they deem necessary."*

Pay close attention to what expenses you are responsible for and whether or not you have the ability to approve them in advance.

5. Most agreements will also have direct verbiage relating to the **Exclusivity** of your arrangement.

> *"The retention of Intermediary hereunder as advisor to Client with respect to this engagement shall be on an exclusive basis. In order to coordinate the efforts of this process, neither Client nor any management or representatives will initiate discussions regarding a possible transaction with any interested parties except through Intermediary."*

Although the language may seem a little strong at first glance, business owners have to realize there can only

be one "captain of the ship." While you maintain all decision-making authority, the intermediary must know that all negotiations pass through him. Without this exclusivity, it is impossible to track all that is being agreed upon and disseminated.

6. Finally, you should always insure that anyone you are discussing confidential information with has executed a confidentiality agreement that prohibits him or her from **Disclosure.**

> *"Intermediary agrees not to use and to hold in strict confidence all proprietary, secret, or confidential information learned by Intermediary during this term for a period of three years from the date of this agreement, except information that is in the public domain, or subsequently made public, or at the time of disclosure already in the possession of Intermediary. Client hereby authorizes Intermediary to communicate all public and confidential information to interested parties who have signed a confidentiality agreement."*

Make sure your intermediary is bound by a confidentiality agreement both during the agreement and a subsequent survival period. The intermediary must have the ability to release information once a confidentiality agreement has been signed on the part of the prospective purchaser.

After making a decision to sell your company, the next most important decision is who to hire to assist you. Your focus should be on hiring a firm that matches your desires, not hiring a firm and then attempting to shape them to fit your needs. Now that you understand the benefits of using an intermediary, what to look for in an intermediary, and the basic terms of an engagement agreement, you can confidently advance to the next step in the process: pre-sales planning.

Section II

Pre-Sale Planning

Chapter 4
Need Analysis

An experienced mountain climber knows pre-climb planning is every bit as important as skilled maneuvering during the ascent itself. As a result, the climber defines where he is going, how he will get there, and anticipates the challenges he'll face along the way. He prepares strategies for dealing with hazards and makes careful plans to avoid pitfalls. Finally, the climber will constantly monitor the environment (i.e. weather) in which he will be performing.

When selling a business, intense preparation and planning is imperative. Just as a novice climber would never tackle a mountain without a guide, a business owner should recognize that an experienced advisor and well thought out approach are keys to a successful transaction.

The first step in preparing a business for sale is need analysis. You must be able to answer the question, "What am I going to accomplish and why?" The only reason to embark on an endeavor is to achieve something of value. So, what do you hope to realize? Is there some place that you want to be that is different than where you are today?

At the most basic level, the business exists to serve the needs and desires of the business owner or owners (and

their dependents/loved-ones). Every company was formed by an owner as a means by which personal needs and desires could be obtained, such as income, freedom, self-actualization, or a better future. Alternately, to be a successful venture, the owner must focus on the wants of the customers, employees, vendors, - everyone but himself or herself. Throughout the process, however, the business owner's personal needs must be attained, or why own the business?

In addition, the needs of any particular business owner may change over time. Often, goal alterations cause the business owner to decide to sell. If a business was formed as a means to create financial security for its founder, there may come a day when that initial goal has been sufficiently satisfied. Mission accomplished. The business owner will then have to find new motivation for his hard work and trouble or else he should decide to sell.

Sometimes values change due to external factors, such as health challenges. How enticing is working to achieve your dreams when the work load is causing you health problems that jeopardize your life!

Analyzing an owner's motivating factors may also help explain the relationship conflicts characteristically encountered between founder and successor. For example, the prototypical founder spent his adult life fighting to secure and retain financial security, while his son has always enjoyed financial comfort. The son may not share the urgency to maintain security. Without ever having experienced the pain of poverty, the son may be

more concerned with quality of life, recognition, hobbies, or the environment. Viewed in this light, it is easy to see how two generations can have trouble communicating.

Case in Point: Mr. Smith, a 74-year-old client, bought into a small fabrication business thirty-five years ago. Mr. Smith grew up poor, dreamed of independence and wealth, and trusted that hard work and frugality would ensure his success. It did. Over the years he bought out his two partners using money saved through his frugality. As a result, the business netted around $1,000,000 annually. Though the owner attained financial security, he still believed in the principles that got him there - hard work and frugality.

Conversely, his son worked in the business managing a facility in another town. Mr. Smith gave up trying to get his son to take over the business and hired an intermediary to facilitate the business sale. Mr. Smith could not understand why his son was so lazy.

What the father did not comprehend was that the son had amassed a very comfortable retirement fund through the company's generous retirement savings plan. The son's financial house was secure, especially with his anticipated inheritance from his elderly father's sizeable estate. Furthermore, the son did not wish to bear the headaches of running the entire business or the financial and relationship stress of buying out his father. In addition, he did not want to move his wife and children away from their home community.

When we consider the previously mentioned case from a need analysis standpoint, the explanation for the conflict in values between the owner and his son is evident. People do what makes sense in their own lives, not the lives of others. Everyone's goals differ; therefore, their actions differ.

Before one begins the process of selling a business, the owner must first define his or her ultimate goal. Personal issues drive the business sale decision. It is important to ask at the onset, "What, on a personal level, are you trying to accomplish in the sale of your business, Mr. Seller?" Below are examples of actual, properly formed, and specific need analysis statements. Each owner is very clear in what he or she wants to accomplish on an individual level:

> *"I can't keep working this hard. I am experiencing health problems and need to slow down."*

> *"I don't enjoy my job anymore. I'm sick of the employee hassles and turnover. I am burned out and need to make a change."*

> *"My business is struggling financially and I'm scared that it might fail. I don't want to lose any more of the financial wealth that I have built."*

> *"My key, long-time general manager has resigned. I can't run this business without him."*

"Competition is getting stiffer and stiffer. Consolidation in my industry is creating huge competitors with significant resources and power. The future does not look bright for a small company like mine."

"I am 70-years-old and should get my house in order so that if I passed away or became ill, my business does not suffer and my wife is not left with a headache. Besides, my wife and I want some years to travel and relax."

"My business is on such an upswing, everything seems to be going right. I don't know if there will ever be a better time to sell. You know what they say, buy low, sell high."

"I inherited this business from my father. I never really wanted to be a business person, but always felt that it was my duty to take over the family business. I am not happy. I want to finally do what I want, which is move to Florida and be a fishing guide."

None of the need analysis statements mention selling the business. They should not. The point is to isolate the values of the owner. Selling a business is a solution to a

problem, not the goal itself. Once the owner completes the need analysis and then writes down his or her main motivating factors, he or she can then begin considering alternatives.

Ask yourself, "What actions could be taken that might solve my problem or address my need"? An owner should find the solution or action that meets the demand with the fewest negative effects and lowest cost and risk.

After evaluating your personal goals, a qualified intermediary is invaluable. Often times the business owner does not see other solutions for meeting his or her objectives. Again, selling the company is just one solution — a pretty drastic one.

Let's take a look at one of the need analysis statements presented in the prior section and brainstorm as to potential solutions:

> "I don't enjoy my job anymore. I'm sick of the employee hassles and turnover. I am burned out, and need to make a change."

Solution Alternatives:
- Reduce workload by delegating more tasks
- Delegate the human resources or managerial tasks, which may not be your strength
- Take an occasional vacation or two months off very soon

- Begin stress-reducing activities
- Change your business model to one that uses more automated processes rather than high numbers of employees
- Sell a business unit that is the cause of most of the headaches
- Sell the entire company
- Hire or promote someone to manage the entire company

It is important in this solution analysis stage to consider any and all possible solutions and to write them down. It is a good idea to include other people at this step since different perspectives often bring alternate ideas. Again, the goal is to find the action that meets the need with the fewest negative effects, lowest possible cost, and minimal risk.

Furthermore, put each idea on a separate piece of paper. Add an "attributes", "detriments" and "costs" column. Take the time to fully analyze each answer. The owner should allow weeks or even months for this process to re-consider each alternative and make repeated adjustments to the attributes, detriments and costs. Once the highest and best solution is found, a mission statement should be written.

Here are examples of actual mission statements written by sellers:

> "*Reduce my work load, stress level, and number or hours worked per week by*

43

delegating more tasks to my employees."

"Respond to the rising competition level in my industry by selling to a major consolidator while my value is still intact and the buyers are still paying top dollar."

"Become a fishing guide in Florida. To enable me to do such, I will sell my business to relieve me from the demands of owning and running it and to provide me with the cash I'll need."

Once the seller has clearly identified what he or she wishes to accomplish on a personal level, the owner should establish specific goals relating to the business. Assuming that the chosen solution is to sell the business, common goals involve price, deal terms, and a timeline. Other goals might include the retention of a key employee after divestiture or the maintenance of the present headquarters location. Here is an example of properly formulated goals for a proposed sale transaction:

1. Total sale price of $10,000,000 with no less than $7,000,000 in cash at closing.
2. Credited and trustworthy buyer (as long as a material amount is seller-financed).
3. Deal closed by July 1st.
4. Maintain confidentiality. Only John and

Carol should become aware that the business may sell. In no case should customer A or B become aware during the process.
5. Revenues and profits continue on budget through deal closing.

As a business owner, you understand the value of a clearly defined plan and strategy. This is even more important when contemplating the sale of your company. Just as a well-developed marketing plan can do wonders for the expansion of your business, a well thought out exit strategy, with written goals and values, is essential to the divestiture of your business and achievement of your long-term goals.

It is important to note, however, that the marketplace significantly dictates price and terms. Proper preparation, professional packaging, thorough buyer search, and experienced negotiating skills are a necessity. But once these elements are in place, the market will greatly determine price and terms. Before you can estimate an accurate sales price for your business, you must first get an accurate idea of your business value.

Common Pitfall:
Contact with potential buyers before determining game plan: Seller decides that he wants to sell, then he impulsively approaches his peer, key supplier, or lead employee to discuss the possibility. Completely ill prepared and not even knowing what price is fair or if

his desire is enduring, the owner will most likely encounter strained relationships and lost credibility.

Chapter 5
Determining Business Value

Before any sales effort is undertaken, the seller should have a good understanding of the prices being paid for comparable companies and what is reasonable to expect. Additionally, it is important to identify what certain buyers are looking for and how to properly distribute requested company information.

Volumes of books explain how to properly assess a business. Knowledge of valuation methodology is important, but equally significant is present information on the price and terms at which deals are being done currently in the marketplace. Industry specific data is most useful. Over the past decade, the availability of data on private company sales has improved substantially.

Most intermediaries have access to databases that provide details on recent business sale transactions. Seller representatives, without revealing identities, provide transaction data. Trade associations and public company acquisitions are two other good sources of market data information. Dogged research may also turn up some actual sale transaction data. Just remember that hearsay is almost always flawed and should not be relied upon.

So what drives business value? Below is a list of characteristics that potentially drive higher values and generally lead to increased sale prices. Conversely, the lack of such features in a business will detract from market value. To the extent that these elements are improved in a particular business, the market value of the business is improved.

Growth Rate: The growth rate of sales and profits compared to our national growth rate and the growth rate of the company's particular industry. Higher growth rates command higher values.

Operating Profits: Higher profits as a percent of sales compared to industry averages. Operating profit margins that exceed industry averages will command higher values.

Management Quality and Depth: Depth, quality, tenure, experience, success record, education, as well as succession for managers and key employees. Above average management and employees will reduce risk during transition and justify higher multiples.

Niche, Market Position, Brand Awareness and Identity: If a company fills a definable niche, commands a special leadership position, or has strong and favorable brand awareness in their market - whether for products, services, geographic areas, production efficiencies or certain capabilities – a higher value should be supported.

Multiple Customer Groups: If the product or service offerings of a company have multiple customer groups, markets, or end users, a higher value is justified. This usually means there are various opportunities for growth through entering or further penetrating new markets.

Proprietary Products: The more proprietary the products, the higher the profit potential and value. For example, a non-exclusive distributor enjoys little differentiation or protection from pricing pressure. However, a manufacturer of a proprietary line of products should enjoy a more defensible market position.

Customers: Diversification of customers, their length of time buying from the company, as well as their financial strength and payment history are important considerations when assessing a business. What would the impact on the company be if the largest customer were lost? If the answer is very little, then the company has virtually no customer concentration risk and can command a higher value.

Product Mix and Gross Profit: The greater the number of products the company sells and the greater the gross profit on each line, the stronger the case for a higher valuation.

Condition and Appearance of Tangible Assets: Does the business "show well"? Is it attractive in appearance? Is the facility clean, painted, and bright? What is the age and

condition of the productive assets? Does the office appear clean and organized or cluttered and unprofessional?

Replacement Value of Assets: Viewing the business from the eyes of the buyer, how much money would it cost to duplicate the assets, infrastructure, personnel, systems, and customers of the company? Don't forget to consider patents and other intangible assets, favorable leases, or agreements.

Interim Results: Buyers are interested in what the business will do in the future. The best indication is the present. Strong current performance can justify higher prices, whereas a dip in performance will always put a drag on pricing.

Growth Capacity: If the existing employees, working capital, facilities, and systems are adequate to support the projected growth over the next few years, a higher than average valuation will be supported. List the level of revenues that the business, without additional investments or hiring, could support. What would be the limiting resource at that level? What would be the second bottleneck and what would it cost to relieve each of the bottlenecks?

Projections: The higher and more certain the projected sales and cash flow of the business, the higher the multiple of trailing cash flow.

Overall Reputation in the Community and Industry: Healthy and favorable reputations make doing business easier. As a result of a positive reputation, you can attract higher quality employees, win customers more easily, and attract better service and terms from vendors. Is the company's reputation strong, or have they burned bridges and worn out their welcome within the community?

Quality of Financial Information: Financial statements present the financial health and performance of a company. Audited financial reports by a well-known and independent audit firm are the highest quality statements. Reviewed statements by a similar type firm would be the second preference.

Absence of Risk: Risk and uncertainty lower value. If a company has existing or pending litigation, potential environmental issues, a reputation for being litigious, is in a changing or threatened market niche, or possesses other risk factors, value will decline.

This list is not meant to be all-inclusive, but it is fairly comprehensive in scope and touches on the key areas of value and risk typically investigated and considered by middle-market buyers. Having more of these values certainly helps you raise the value of a business; however, these benefits are balanced by any risk factors. If you want to increase the value of your business, lower the risk to the buyer. Of course, another real issue is *perceived* risk and emotion.

Successful and experienced sales professionals realize major purchase decisions are emotional not logical. Business sales are no different. Experienced intermediaries know that companies are rarely sold based solely on the numbers, but on the fit with the buyer or other more subjective criteria.

True, the fundamentals must work. In addition, if a bank is involved, cash flow is important. However, buyers need to see how your company will solve their specific needs. For example, if a car buyer has small children and is concerned about reliability, a good car salesman will focus on the safety features of a vehicle. Similarly, the business seller should listen carefully to the driving factors of each buyer and market to those characteristics.

Case in Point: A wealthy Texas industrialist was deep into prolonged negotiations to buy a Russian manufacturing firm. The two sides remained several million dollars apart. The Russian seller was savvy and had come to know the Texan well. He invited the Texan to visit one last time to try and work the deal out. The seller was asking $15 million, while the buyer wanted to pay no more than $13 million. After a day of meetings, the two went to dinner. The buyer still had not budged on his price. It appeared the deal was going to die.

It was common in Russia to build monuments and for businesses to display the statues of their founders out front. Late in the evening, the seller

offered to sell for $14.75 million and build a 17-foot statue of the new Texas owner (at the cost of $25,000) in front of the building. Done deal.

Chapter 6
Tax Planning and Offering Documents

Not only is it important to understand how to calculate true business value, it is also vital to plan for the tax ramifications of a business sale. Before pursuing any discussions with buyers, the seller should plan in advance a strategy to maximize profits and provide a smooth transition.

Alternative deal structures will impact after-tax sale proceeds. Benefits and detriments to different types of sales are discussed in depth in Section V. An intermediary as well as a tax specialist, whether an accountant or lawyer, can be reliable sources for tax issue analysis - just make sure you work with an advisor that has transaction experience.

After creating an effective post-sale tax strategy, it is important to prepare your deal book containing offering documents. Four key offering documents must be prepared in advance of any contact with buyers:

1. Confidentiality Agreement
2. Confidential Offering Memorandum

3. Generic Summary
4. Supplemental Information Package

1. The **Confidentiality Agreement** is a critical document of the sale process. There is risk inherent in providing confidential data to third parties. The purpose of the confidentiality agreement is to limit how such information can be used. The key elements of any confidentiality agreement are as follows:

- Buyer identification
- Statement saying information provided is confidential and sensitive
- Buyer's agreement to not disclose identify of seller to any other persons without permission from seller or seller's representative
- Buyer's agreement to use information only to evaluate business for purchase
- Buyer's agreement that if buyer decides not to pursue a purchase of business, all information will be returned to seller or seller's representative
- Instructions to buyer regarding contact person for questions, how and when
- Buyer's agreement that in the event of breaches of agreement, buyer will be liable for any damages
- Binding signature of authorized buyer representative

2. **Confidential Offering Memorandum:** The purpose of the offering memorandum is to help interested

parties understand your business, including its strengths, weaknesses, and potential. It should be clear, professional, visual, simple, and easy to read. It should also provide the facts of the business accurately. Highly sensitive information may be held out – such as customer, supplier, and employee names. This type of data is not necessary for the buyer to gather a good understanding of the business.

Buyer candidates should receive the offering document only after they have been properly screened, agreed to the terms of the release of such information (verbally and in writing), and after receiving a brief oral description of the business. By using an oral description to eliminate poor buyer candidates, the seller and intermediary will spend far less time chasing low probability deals and invest more time with highly viable buyers.

Counter to the mentality of a salesperson, the process of selling a business is as much one of eliminating buyers as finding buyers. An intermediary is looking for the very best buyer candidate, while reducing the potential of harming the business during the process. The journey is one of identifying as many good buyer candidates as possible, then quickly eliminating unqualified prospects while disclosing as little about the seller's business as possible. In a typical offering, only a handful of qualified buyers will receive the confidential offering document, but those few are very strong candidates.

The confidential offering document should be

written with the buyer in mind. It should provide the buyer with the information that he or she needs to evaluate the opportunity from their perspective. Every business is unique and the logical buyer candidates differ with each seller project. As such, the information contained in the offering document will differ. Here is the basic data that most should contain:

- Business history
- Ownership history
- Current ownership and legal structure
- Products and services
- Key employees
- Marketing and sales methods and processes
- Customer types
- Vendors
- Industry served and industry trends
- Competitive landscape and key competitors or peers
- Sales and income history
- Recasting of income statements
- Current balance sheet
- Recasting of balance sheet
- Key contracts and agreements, if any
- Off-balance sheet assets and liabilities
- Recent capital expenditures or investments
- Descriptions of facilities and lease or purchase options
- Employee benefits programs and personnel policies

- Growth opportunities
- Seller's reason for selling
- Terms of offering

3. Generic Summary: The generic summary is a tool for attracting buyer candidates. To determine whether the business may meet a buyer's criteria, a generic summary provides basic data about the company, but not enough information to discern the identity of the offered business. This is a delicate balance, with caution falling on the side of non-disclosure. Simple data on the size and industry sector (manufacturing or distribution) will allow buyers to screen themselves. Common information included in the generic summary is:

- Brief description of products and/or service
- Location(s) of business (generally)
- Sales and owner earnings, brief historical summary
- Balance sheet, current recast summary
- Reason for sale

Note: The income presented in the generic summary should be recast, or "owner earnings". An in-depth explanation of how to recast financial statements is provided in Chapter 7.

In the sale process buyers do not appear, they must be located. By limiting a candidate list to buyers

you already identify in advance, you may be doing yourself a disservice. By promoting the generic summary to a wide audience that may not specifically fit a hypothetical profile, you open yourself up to the possibility of a nice surprise - a great buyer that was not anticipated. The generic summary can be advertised on a web site or direct mailing. A good buyer may be found this way with little risk.

The generic summary also helps in the screening process. Once a buyer is interested, the seller or seller's representative has leverage to obtain the basic information necessary to screen the buyer and protect the seller.

To protect the seller, several issues need to be addressed with the buyer candidate.

- Does the buyer have sufficient resources and high enough interest to merit the risks inherent in disclosure?
- What relationships or abilities of the buyer candidate make them either benign or dangerous?
- Is there agreement on the terms of disclosure?

Of course, most sellers would not present the questions in this raw form. Most intermediaries would gently gather the necessary data through a comfortable dialogue with the buyer. If the buyer resists, he or she may need to be reminded of the sensitive nature of the data as well as the risks to the owners and their loved

ones. If the buyer refuses to accommodate, the seller should conclude that the buyer is either unqualified, unreasonable, or has ulterior motives.

The owner, in his or her desire to sell, should not provide sensitive information to unqualified or uncooperative persons. Remember, the seller has all the strength at this point because he or she does not have to agree to move forward until the buyer provides the necessary information. If done correctly, it is possible to manage this process in a friendly, professional, and respectful manner. A professional intermediary should have the experience and skills to manage this delicate process.

4. Supplemental Package contains information held back for confidentiality reasons, information necessary to back-up summary data provided in the offering memorandum, and items expected to be requested during due diligence. *This data should only be provided after agreement on a term sheet.* A term sheet is discussed at length in Section IV. A supplemental package will commonly contain the following:

- Copies of key contracts or agreements germane to the business
- Copies of leases
- Copies of borrowing agreements (if a stock sale is contemplated)
- Customer list

- Vendor list
- Original annual financial statements (4 years plus year-to-date)
- Monthly income statements (past 3 years)
- Federal tax returns (past 4 years)
- Current depreciation schedule
- Copy of documentation evidencing key intangible assets, such as certifications, patents or copyrights
- Employee list
- Employee handbook (or similar policy writing)
- Accounts receivable aging
- Accounts payable aging
- Inventory list
- Buy-sell agreement, if one exists
- Articles of incorporation, operating agreement, stockholder agreement (if such is pertinent to sale)

Today, legal agreements are often signed as a formality without first being read and understood. The seller should make very clear, through personal communication with the buyer, that the confidentiality agreement is not a mere formality. The seller should make sure the buyer reads the agreement in its entirety, understands the terms, and has answers to any questions. It should be clear that the breach and harm provisions will be enforced and a copy should be provided to the buyer.

After qualifying a select number of key buyers and getting agreement on non-disclosure terms, a seller should recast the income statements to present his company to the best possible advantage.

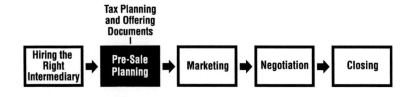

Chapter 7
Recasting Income Statements and Balance Sheets

Recasting the historical income statements is critical when selling a business. Buyers of private companies, especially individual buyers, are interested in the total benefits they will generate for themselves if they buy the business. The historical net profits of the business, as presented on the company income statements or tax returns, may not accurately reflect the complete benefits enjoyed by the owner and may be a poor surrogate for future profit potential. By recasting, we adjust the historical financial statements as follows:

- **Non-Recurring Expenses**: Eliminate those expenses that burdened the historical profits, but are not expected to do so in the future.
- **Unnecessary Expenses:** Eliminate those costs that affect the historical profits, but that are not necessary for the operation of the business going forward.
- **Owner Benefits**: Add back to net profit the total dollar value of all benefits received by the owner.

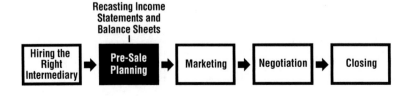

Non-Recurring Expenses are expenses that were incurred in the past that will not or should not be incurred in the future. For example, a distributor spent significant dollars two years ago pursuing the rights to distribute a new product line, legal fees to negotiate the agreement, and travel costs to send his salesperson to be trained. The company expensed the costs when incurred, so the profits of the business were burdened by this one time only expense. As in any future business investment, the expenses precluded the future profitability. Today, the owner is reaping great profits without the burden of past expenses.

If the buyer looked at the unadjusted historical profit performance of the business to estimate the future profits, it is likely that projections would be understated. Because the strongest driver of value is profits, it is in the best interest of the seller to provide a recast profit statement that will show the non-recurring expense. Recasting the income statement will highlight what the profits would have been had this expense not been incurred, and provide a better indication of the true profitability of business as it relates to the future.

Unnecessary Expenses are expenses not required for the profitable operation of the business. The assumption is that a buyer will maximize profits going forward. If a future buyer can eliminate an unnecessary expense, such expenditure should not have a detrimental impact on value. Some examples include an airplane that is owned by the business but not necessary, an employee that is kept out of friendship rather than productivity, or a money-losing product line that is kept because it is owned by the son of

the owner. All of these items could be eliminated after the sale of the company.

Owner Benefits are when the reported profits of the business do not show the monetary benefits the owner enjoys. In recasting, it is common to add the sum of all seller benefits, such as salary, health and medical expenses, life insurance expenses, retirement plan contributions, automobile(s), and cell phones. Included can also be personal expenses paid by the business, exurbanite or unnecessary payroll costs (such as a loved one whose actual contribution to the business is less that their pay), unnecessary travel, or hobby costs. Any expenses that serve the owner rather than the business can be considered "owner benefit" and added back to profits.

Such expenses are common in private businesses. One significant reason is the United States tax laws, which tax the reported profits of businesses to a very high level. To the extent that a business owner can obtain personal benefits in the form of deductible expenses, they have obtained personal "income" in a pre-tax basis. This practice is illegal, but common.

The purpose for recasting the business balance sheet is altogether different than the purpose of recasting income statements. Balance sheets are simply a listing of business assets and with fair values. The assessments are supposed to reflect the true economic value to the business, whether it is positive or negative. Accounting rules are designed to enhance the likelihood that balance sheets provide an accurate representation.

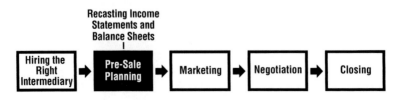

However, balance sheets rarely reflect the true fair market value of the assets and liabilities of a business. This is due to inherent limitations to accepted accounting practices, failure of many businesses to understand and/or adhere to accepted accounting practices, and tax laws that skew balance sheet values. Regardless of the reasons, a buyer needs to know the true value of the assets he is purchasing and the liabilities that he is assuming. As a result, the seller needs to make sure that all of the business assets for sale are listed on the balance sheet with accurate values. Recasting of the balance sheet ignores accounting rules and simply attempts to list assets and liabilities at their true fair market values.

Once you have recast the income statements and balance sheets, you need to put on the finishing touches before marketing your company for sale. The final step in preparing a business for sale is to give your company a proper "wax job". For example, when you sell a car, it makes sense to polish the outside and vacuum the inside. When the car has proper maintenance papers and it shows well, it will receive a higher price. The same principal holds true for the sale of a business. Before a potential buyer walks through your front door, you want to make sure the business shows well. The first impression is important.

Almost every business has things that could be done to improve the visual appeal of the facilities. With very little expense, an owner could repair a fence, wax the floor, or clean the trucks and equipment. In addition, updating advertisements and sales brochures help create a great first

impression. Finally, organize the work and office areas. The buyer will consider the employees unmotivated and the company unorganized if the company has lots of clutter.

As you can see, selling a company requires numerous pre-sales planning steps before taking it to market. After a seller has identified his or her personal objectives, created a successful post-sale tax strategy, prepared proper offering documents, recast the income statements and balance sheets, and given his company a "cleaning up", he or she will be in a much better position to attract maximum value for the business.

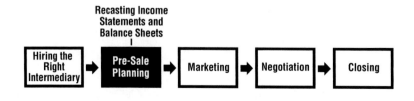

Section III

Marketing

Chapter 8
Buyer Types

As with pre-sales planning, there are many factors to consider before you can design an effective marketing strategy. An owner must first prepare mentally and emotionally for the process, profile the hypothetical buyer types, be ready to generate and manage buyer interest, and have a method of comparing offers. Broad databases, compelling offering memorandums, and great buyer search tools all help to find a buyer, but understanding the human element and emotional factors that motivate different types of buyers are equally important.

A couple of mental framing elements are helpful in the process of finding a buyer. First, begin with the end in mind. Most owners go to the market with the idea they are hoping to find a buyer, get an offer or offers, and cash out. To mentally prepare for a successful transaction, however, requires a paradigm shift.

Every business is one of a kind. An owner spends significant energy on creating a highly transferable company, so it is important to **choose** the buyer. In the end, the owner will need to decide to whom he will sell the company. By profiling the ideal buyer in advance, a seller will avoid many merger or sale disasters. Pitfalls involve

losing key customers, alienating top employees, disrupting the business workflow, and seeing all of your hard work in building a company destroyed by selling to the wrong buyer.

Case in Point: A private equity group acquired a $75,000,000 group of companies. A retiring entrepreneur with a strong management team led the largest of the acquired companies. Since strategically fitting in the top managers into the deal looked too difficult, the sellers paid little attention to the future plans of the buyer. The owners cashed out with 90% cash and 10% promissory note.

Rather than promote from within, the private equity group recruited a CEO, CFO and COO from outside the industry. Within one year of ownership, the new management group had broken multiple principles of the past companies as well as introduced new manufacturing techniques that the work force never accepted. Due to a lack of confidence in management, the middle mangers began to defect. As the private equity group struggled to replace management, the company fell into Chapter 11 bankruptcy. The original companies were each individually auctioned off.

Avoiding this type of situation is one of the main reasons to hire a professional intermediary. A good intermediary has extensive experience not only in finding buyers that are a good match to the seller, but also in negotiating issues which may seem like impossible stumbling blocks to an owner.

The first step in finding the right buyer is understanding the different types of buyers and the characteristics of each.

Buyer Types

Buyers can be grouped into three main types: **individual**, **financial**, and **strategic**.

1. Individual buyers are characterized by persons looking for a "job" as well as an investment. They typically want the business to be near where they live or at least limited to where their wife and family are willing to relocate. Individual buyers are more emotional, desire businesses that fit with their particular experience or relationships, and often have limited equity capital to invest. These buyers often rely on raising the necessary capital and will respond well to higher levels of hand holding and seller support. Many have never purchased or sold a business previously.

2. Financial buyers are experienced, well-capitalized business corporations who are focused on healthy financial returns. Such buyers may be wealthy individuals, families, or investor groups. They typically do not work directly in the business, rather they back an industry veteran to run the business or they rely on retaining existing management. Such buyers are less emotional, tend not to pay premiums, and are more flexible in location.

3. Strategic or **synergistic buyers** are also referred to as industry buyers or financial partners. This buyer is motivated by synergies that may exist between the target company and a company or companies already owned by the buyer. The synergies may be simply from scale or volume, vertical integration, process, or technology. Great caution should be used in working with industry buyers, as they are often in a position to use data in a way that could harm the seller's business.

These financial partners or private equity groups (PEGs) are typically companies with skeleton staffs that focus on buying and selling companies into their portfolio. A better way to describe these buyers would be to call them a conglomerate of unconnected middle market companies.

Wealthy individuals or fund managers typically create these companies with a central focus on growth and return on investment. Most often they will have a stated criteria for the platform companies. The majority will focus on manufacturing companies or value-added distributors. It is estimated that there are more than 1,000 active private equity groups in the United States. In addition, there are many other groups, such as venture capitalists, equity funds and angel investors, that invest in or buy companies.

An owner does not have to sell 100% of a business to meet his objectives. A company can sell 20% to 100% of its ownership, allow the owner to cash out, get additional growth capital, and protect the interest of significant stake holders. This type of flexibility allows for creative deals.

Case in Point: A father, a son, and son-in-law who were both active in a business as well as two non-active daughters, owned ABC company. Thirty percent of the stock had already been gifted or purchased by the siblings and Dad was ready to retire. Dad felt obligated to clean up his finances by cashing out the non-active daughters, but the sons wanted to stay as management and retain their ownership. The perfect buyer was a financial group. The father and non-active daughters were bought out. The son replaced his father as CEO and now, 9 years later, the company has doubled in size and quadrupled in profits. Even though the son has a minority interest, he now has industry leaders on his board of directors.

    Each type of buyer (individuals, corporate, or financial groups) will be as unique as the owner's personal goals and objectives. Each buyer type responds differently and buys for different reasons. Smart sellers know whom they are dealing with and act accordingly. One specific buyer type or possibly all three types of buyers may fit the criteria and goals of a seller. Many owners naturally rule out the individual buyer. However, there could be a special individual that is positioned to pay more and do a much better job of running your business than a financial group. It is important to be open-minded to buyer options.

    After you have a better understanding of the types of buyers, you are ready to create a marketing strategy of profiling key buyer types, generating buyer interest, managing buyer interest, and closing the deal.

Chapter 9
Buyer Profiles

Before diving into the implementation of a marketing plan, it is important to create a buyer profile. This may seem burdensome, but a short cut could have serious ramifications down the road.

Case in Point: A telephone sales and service company decided to sell. Of the $3.8 million revenue, more than half originated from one customer. That customer had just been purchased and announced they would bring their telephone services inside the organization. This set the criteria for a buyer as a group or individual that had strong marketing and sales skills and the ability to build on the remaining base of customers.

The business was sold for the standalone value of the assets, plus a small note with very favorable terms. The business had been severely discounted because of the loss of the major customer. According to his resume, the new owner was a marketing and sales management-type with a great history in building companies for other people. The seller did not investigate the non-financial references and background of the buyer. An investigation of the buyer's background would have revealed that he had been fired

from each previous position for lack of performance and had blamed his failure on outside influences or management's misrepresentations.

After his first anniversary of owning the business, the new owner had yet to write a marketing plan, build a sales force, or even attempt to find additional customers. A frivolous lawsuit was filed claiming the seller had falsely represented future revenues - a claim that had no basis. The lesson learned: move slowly and deliberately and don't take short cuts. Even a cash deal can turn into wasted time and expense after the sale.

So, what is really important in the qualification process? Financial research is important, but it is equally important to determine the reasons a buyer is interested. The following is an all too common scenario:

After marketing the sale of a business through advertising and direct mail, the seller gets a phone call. The party on the other end of the phone has received a letter with the general summary. He is interested in the company and would like more information. The seller faxes a confidentiality agreement, the prospect signs it, and then faxes it back. A confidential offering memorandum is then overnighted to the prospect.

Although it seems to be a logical system, there are some potential pitfalls. For example, what steps were taken to qualify the buyer prior to offering the confidentiality agreement? The seller may request that the buyer candidate provide proof of financial capacity. Many days or even weeks can be spent negotiating to receive a financial

statement or a bank reference and exactly what do you have with either?

If a seller has no idea what the prospective buyer is thinking or how the seller's business fits into the prospect's business plan, he may waste significant time with the wrong candidate. Qualification of a buyer should include matching the goals and direction of the seller's company with the profile of the buyer prospect's company and the melding of their vision and plans for the future.

To fully understand the type of buyer that will fit into your company, it is important to first profile your own business. By sketching out a simple **SWOT** (strengths, weaknesses, opportunities, and threats) analysis of your business, you can find a buyer that offsets your weaknesses.

Case in Point: A firm is highly competent in designing, developing, and getting products to the market. However, a competitor with huge market share continually copies or knocks off the new products before the firm can reach critical mass in the marketplace.

Weakness #1: The firm is not financially capable of capitalizing on their innovation and thereby fully enjoying the fruits of this valuable capability.

Weakness #2: The company's sales and staff is not large enough to reach the market before the competition reacts.

Illustration of SWOT summary

Strengths
Design & development of top quality products
Speed of products to the market
Efficient production facilities and work force
Extra capacity
Clear vision of customer future needs

Weaknesses
Large market to reach
Current market share small
Under capitalized
Lack of a well financed marketing team and distribution system

Opportunities
Add dealers
Take products through other distribution channels
Use design engineering to enter allied industry
Customize products specifically to small niche markets
Cut freight cost with production on East and West coast

Threats
Well financed competitors copy our products
Products are "effectively" non-patentable
Engineers and design people could be recruited by competitors

    Since we have identified the company's SWOT, it is easy to see how the ideal buyer would fit into the previous example. If this firm were to find the perfect individual buyer, how would

the buyer look? Consider the following abbreviated chart when profiling an individual buyer or corporate management team:

TRAITS AND BEHAVIORS

Introverted	1	5	10
Extroverted	1	5	10
Pragmatic	1	5	10
Analytical	1	5	10
Patience	1	5	10
Energy level	1	5	10

SKILLS & ABILITIES

Sales	1	5	10
Marketing	1	5	10
Recruiting	1	5	10
Networking skills	1	5	10
Financial management	1	5	10
Creativity	1	5	10
Accounting	1	5	10
Negotiations	1	5	10

CONTACTS & EXPERIENCES

Industry experience	1	5	10
Distribution relationships	1	5	10
Industry contacts	1	5	10
Innovative design experience	1	5	10
Systems development experience	1	5	10
Product development experience	1	5	10
Leadership structures experience	1	5	10
FINANCIAL STRENGTH	1	5	10

Assuming an individual buys the company, which factors are the most important according to the weaknesses described? The most important elements in the previous example are strong financial abilities, industry contacts, network, distribution relationships, and recruiting ability.

What about marketing to the second type of buyer, the financial buyer or corporation? It is much easier to assume that an existing distribution channel already in place can strengthen these weaknesses with a competitor or a company in a similar industry, but that is not always the case. The slow and lumbering giants can sometimes be so set in their processes that expanding to your product line or service becomes nearly impossible. When looking into both corporate and financial partners, it is important to consider these additional characteristics:

Corporate Compatibility
Cultural compatibility
Roles to be played by seller's management team
Leadership style
Ability to recognize and pay full value for your company
Honesty, integrity, fairness, and trust

Process Compatibility
Accounting systems
Sales systems management and territory overlay
Operations, JIT, ISO9002, cell production
Product compatibility
Market synergies

After evaluating the buyer type and characteristics that would complement your company, you can begin to seriously consider the buyers you should be targeting and begin to implement a marketing plan. The profile stimulates the creation of the target list of buyers.

Chapter 10
Generating Buyer Interest

From the profiling process and the SWOT analysis, an outreach marketing strategy will start to emerge. First, an owner and/or intermediary will create two lists: a short list and expanded list. The short list will encompass individuals or companies that the owner or intermediary already has specific knowledge and are easy to profile. This list may include competitors, key management personnel, partners who do not wish to sell, and key customers.

The second list is long and requires more planning and effort to introduce the opportunity to the names on this list. Industry publications, online web-sites, and critical network partners help to create the expanded list. The seller should be involved in each advertising vehicle that will be utilized in the marketing plan. An owner may consider creating a pre-qualification step to limit the time spent on prospects that do not fit with his or her goals and objectives.

Additional names can come from list brokers or large information houses, trade associations, and professional organizations. If it is important to find a local entity to own and operate the business, the local chamber of commerce can also be a great source. It takes a little more creativity when looking for an individual buyer.

87

Case in Point: A Kansas City based custom garment operation had a zero-defect and zero-seconds production reputation and wished to sell the company. Though someone from outside the industry might be capable of taking over the leadership of the firm, the departure of the highly active, well known, and liked (in the industry) seller would create a huge hole for a non-industry buyer.

Though Kansas City was once a large garment hub, times had changed and it was a dying industry. The owner needed to find a buyer that could work on the floor until they could develop qualified middle level managers. The intermediary placed an advertisement in industry trade publications as well as confidentially sought out information on current vendors and competitors. Without disclosing the name of the firm, the advisor identified nine fabric representatives and three thread manufacturers as potential buyers. Two months and numerous contacts later, a ten-year veteran of a large manufacturing plant bought the business.

Once the owner and intermediary have sufficiently brain stormed a list of potential buyers, they can then begin strategizing the proper way to eliminate buyers and the method of approach.

Choices of Approach

There are two basic ways to approach marketing a business for sale: the "**rifle method**" or "**stealth trolling**".

The traditional way of marketing a business is the **rifle method**. This is done by identifying the SIC standard

industrial code (as set forth by the federal government) of the offered company and then contacting all of the companies in and around the same SIC. These contacts are made through mailing a letter and general summary. The generic summary was described in Chapter 6.

Generally, direct mail marketing is far superior to advertising in the newspaper when selling a business. As technology has advanced, fax and Email distribution lists have also become a popular way to get the word out while attempting to preserve confidentiality.

As stated in the previous section, confidentiality is of utmost importance. The normal transaction is kept confidential from the customers, vendors, and employees. Great efforts are made to keep the covert selling activity from leaking back to the people and relationships of the business. Advertisements, Emails, faxes, and summaries are written generically so as not to give away the identity of the company. Conversations are held to a minimum until a non-disclosure is signed.

The second way to approach the sales and marketing effort is called "**stealth trolling**." Another term that could describe stealth trolling would be gorilla networking. This can be done in conjunction with the rifle approach. If you think about this term from the perspective of fishing, it would mean you were trolling for fish with invisible bait. The contact is made with the decision-maker. However, instead of leading with "I got a product", the owner or intermediary focuses on gaining insight into a buyer's plans for the future.

Remember, people don't buy products, they buy

what the product will do for them. In the sale of a business, the old adage about selling the hole the drill makes, not the drill itself holds true. Many sellers fall into the path of least resistance and lead with "would you like to buy a company?" Sometimes this works, but establishing compatibility, communication, and understanding first may be more effective.

Stealth trolling focuses on the intangibles of emotions, goals, and objectives. Driven by a goal-centered approach, the deal will be a much better marriage. Compare this process to a more familiar process – hiring and firing. It is important to hire slowly and fire quickly. For hiring there are numerous models for interviewing, testing, and assessing. In all of the models, the emphasis is on compatibility, skill match, and relational fit.

Just as in hiring an employee, the interview is an important key to finding the best buyer. Whether an interview is done in person or over the phone, the keys to the initial meeting is to screen out candidates who would not be good potential buyers.

Any good interview system is made up of formal questions and responses along with informal essay-type questions. Even though the sale of a business is a much bigger and more important transaction than hiring a person, the interview plan is usually poorly constructed and documented. Unfortunately, the interview process in a sales transaction is too often done without any preparation.

To demonstrate the difference in interviewing using a stealth troll method versus a traditional method, look at the following example:

The Traditional Question Method: Looking for a Buyer:

- I have a company in (or around) your industry for sale. Would you have an interest in growing through acquisition?
- Have you ever bought a business before? Would you be interested in buying one at this point in time?
- Would you be interested in adding over $31 million in sales to your company?
- Have you ever considered merging with another company?
- If you were to look for a perfect merger company, what would it look like?

The Stealth Troll: Looking for a Seller or a Buyer

- Where is your company in its business cycle?
- What is the long-term vision of the company? Who is responsible for carrying it out?
- Have you accomplished every goal you have set for your company?
- What would you add to you firm to make it the strongest in your industry?
- Are you working as smart as you intended to?
- If you had all the money you needed what would you invest it in? What would that do for you?

Can you see a different result coming from the stealth troll? There is no better time to get quality

information and insight than the very first contact. Before they know what you are selling, get the potential buyers to share their feelings about whom they are, where they are, where they are going and the vehicle they are planning on using. This is a place where an intermediary can perform an invaluable service. Intermediaries will generally have previously established relationships with numerous potential buyers that make asking these types of questions easier.

Case in Point: Owner John approached a competitor in an adjacent market. Through minimal research, they found out the competitor was sub-contracting a major piece of his production. In doing so, the competitor's delivery times were double what John could offer as a sub-contractor. The objective of the call was to find out the price they were paying for services and make a proposal to win the business. John was not familiar with the stealth troll method and proceeded with a direct phone call. The call was from owner to owner and went something like this:

> John, "Frank, this is John with XYZ, Inc. I would like to talk to you about the way you do business. "
> Frank, "What does XYZ do?"
> John, "We are in the same business, but we approach it a little differently. That is what I would like to talk to you about."
> Frank, "OK, what do you have in mind?"

John, "I understand you sub-contract to XX company a part of your operation. Is that right?"

Frank, "Yes, we do."

John, "I would like to discuss the opportunities we could create for each other if I were to be your sub-contractor."

Frank, "We use a firm that does not compete in our industry and would never consider giving work to a competitor."

John, "But we are not in the same market, and I think we could both benefit from a relationship."

Frank, "No, I am not interested."

THE END

Two years later John engaged an intermediary to help him acquire similar companies in adjacent markets. One of the first three calls the intermediary made was to Frank. As a third party not connected to the industry, the intermediary could be totally honest and answer all of Frank's questions without giving away the true deal.

The call went something like this:

Intermediary, "Frank, This is xxxx. I am with an international merger and acquisition

company. Do you have a minute?"

Frank, " Possibly, what is this about?"

Intermediary, "I have been working in the YX industry and I wanted to speak with you about where your business is and what you are thinking as it relates to your business and its future.

Frank, "OK? What do you think you can do for me?

Intermediary, "Quite frankly, I don't know. It may be nothing, but if I understand your thinking I will know what to talk to you about."

Frank, "What do you need to know?"

Through a series of questions, Frank expressed:

He is very happy with:
- The way his business operates
- The profitability of the business
- Time off when he wants it for his 12 and 14 year old kids
- Delivery schedule for customers in his market
- His role in customer service

He doesn't want:
- To work any harder or put in any more time
- Production and employee management responsibilities
- Competitors in his market raising delivery expectations

- To invest any more time or money in development

With this basic information, it was clear there could be a fit between John and Frank. In subsequent conversations, these goals and objectives were read back and confirmed by Frank. Now he was ready to hear a proposal for a joint venture. John could build a plant in Frank's geographic area, give Frank a minority ownership interest, and both would have built-in profit from day one.

Whether you use a combination of the rifle approach or stealth trolling, what is most important is finding an effective way to locate and screen your buyers. After you have qualified the long and short list into a targeted group of potential buyers, you are ready to disburse the confidentiality agreement and begin the process of courting buyers.

Chapter 11
Retrieving Confidential Documents and Facility Tours

Two words that normally do not go together when discussing confidential offering memorandums: distribution and retrieval! The confidential offering memorandums go out, but when and how do you get them back? In order to help this process, most intermediaries add a clause to the confidentiality agreement that states:

> *The Prospect will not make copies of the information, and they will return the Confidential Offering Memorandum upon one of two events - they become disinterested, or we request the Confidential Offering Memorandum be returned.*

Most intermediaries handle retrieval of the supplemental package, or due diligence package, in the same way. This package has copies of all the company's leases, contracts, tax returns, and other vital information that needs to be communicated once the other party has qualified themselves as a player or is ready to go into the initial stages of due diligence.

Distributing and retrieving this information can be a very time-consuming process. If an owner is not working with an advisor, this stage can seriously disrupt the owner's current business schedule. Additionally, most owners do not have the time to manage the interest of several key buyers at the same time. This can slow down the process and potentially kill a promising deal. An experienced intermediary should have both the skill and capacity to continually qualify potential buyers, distribute documentation to the right candidates, retrieve and review the documentation, and set up the final stage of marketing: touring the facilities.

Touring the Facility

One successful rule in scheduling meetings and tours with potential buyers is the rule of three. Never make or accept an offer on a business until you have had at least three meetings with the prospect. These meetings can take place over the telephone or in person. Both sides need to go slow. Take your time understanding the other side. All the tools previously described in this section are designed to help you with these principles.

The roles of the seller and buyer are to understand each other's objectives while the role of the intermediary is to facilitate the discussion. If the intermediary talks more than 30% of the time, he has not done a proper job profiling the parties and helping them understand the most important things to discuss.

There is one more role the intermediary needs to fill

- the role of listener. The intermediary should make sure everyone understands exactly what is being said. During these meetings, intent listening is imperative to prevent potential relational hazards.

Case in Point: In the tour and negotiations of a merger between a specialty threaded fastener company (owner #1) and a standard fastener company (owner #2), the owner of the specialty fastener had designed the Confidential Offering Memorandum specifically addressing the issue of control. Owner #1's son was involved in the business but his father had no faith in his ability to take over and run the company. In fact one of the major reasons to merge the company was to create a two-year exit strategy. During the tour and meeting that followed, owner #2 asked about control after merging, and owner #1 responded very clearly regarding his son's abilities.

Two weeks went by without a single telephone call from owner #2. During the follow up call, the intermediary was amazed to find out he had discarded the idea of merging and had just put the Confidential Offering Memorandum in the mail to return it. As the advisor dug deeper, he discovered that there was only one reason for not continuing negotiations. Owner #2 did not want to go to work for owner #1. Even though it was clearly stated in the meeting that owner #1 would not need total ownership or control, owner #2 had it in his head owner #1 would not give it up. Once the discrepancy was discovered, the parties cleared up the misunderstanding and completed the transaction. In fact, their relationship worked so well that

they continued to work together after the expiration of the two-year employment agreement.

Just as a seller and buyer should have certain expectations before meeting in person, an owner should also prepare sufficiently for the facility tours. Every tour should be met with only pleasant surprises. The documentation and telephone communications should communicate a realistic picture of the facilities before the buyer arrives at the company. The tour should be no more than a confirmation of what the prospect was expecting. If they are not, the written and verbal communications need to be reviewed and critiqued to fix the perceptions. Additionally, the owner should take special notice of the cleanliness, organization, and clutter of the facility before entertaining buyers. The first impression of a buyer is critical.

Case in Point: A metal fabrication client did not heed his intermediary's warning and left his facility in poor condition for office tours. As a result, more than fourteen companies decided not to purchase the company due to the dirt on the office floor and apparent lack of productivity by the employees.

It didn't matter that the lease was month to month and the business could be moved to better facilities. Each prospect could not get over the poor condition of the office. In fact, one individual had brought his wife with him. They had no more than crossed the threshold of the front door and the wife leaned over and whispered "You're not buying this company!"

100

One important note while giving facility tours is the need to control the negotiation chatter: the idle "what ifs" that are thrown out during meetings and tours. Most buyers are very good at negotiating as many small details as possible during small talk. Be prepared to do the same. This is when you can learn the way the prospect thinks. How do they treat their employees? What kind of morals and principles carry throughout the organization? When answering their questions, tell them how you feel.

Finally, at the end of the tour, make sure to close with a proper statement, such as "I will look at the overall proposal you give me and address the issues that are most important to you. I am looking for the best relationship first and then we'll work out any price issues."

Planners win and winners plan. Be prepared to go to market and pick the best candidate to own your company. After profiling the best buyer candidate, build the tools and templates necessary to keep you on track during negotiations. At a minimum, create a personal and corporate goals outline and profile the buyer expectations.

Most importantly, do not rush the process. All too often owners go into negotiations without a clear understanding of the purpose of the sale or an outcome expectation. An owner tends to focus on financial issues instead of his or her personal motivations and the right fit for the company. Remember, the fit involves compatibility, communication, understanding, fairness, integrity, and trust between the seller and buyer.

Section IV

Negotiation

Chapter 12
Defining the Negotiation Process

After successfully locating and screening buyer candidates, you are ready to begin the negotiation stage of the process with a few key buyer candidates. This section provides negotiating parties - whether buyer, seller, intermediary or third party professional - with the tools and foundation to successfully navigate through the negotiation journey. Before digging into the fundamentals, it is important to better define negotiation as it relates to mergers, sales and acquisitions.

So, what exactly is negotiation? Depending upon an individual's experience, business culture, and attitude, it can mean confrontation, conflict, and controversy. Conversely, it can mean transition, success and satisfaction. Usually, it lies somewhere on the spectrum between these two extremes.

As a person charts through life, he or she continually experiences and engages in negotiation. During adolescence, a child negotiates for toys, the latest name brand status symbol, and an increased allowance. As adults, a person's focus changes to bigger and more expensive toys,

105

defined values, and possibly financial freedom. Whether the stakes are high or low, satisfaction lies in realizing what ingredients are necessary to secure a favorable outcome.

In the world of business sales and mergers, the stakes are high and the consequences great in victory as well as defeat. Also, winning is not always measured in dollars and cents.

The complexity of negotiation arises from the premise that it is both a science and an art. Scientific or "cookbook" negotiations will advance the parties towards a more meaningful understanding. Whereas, artistic or "intuitive" negotiations cause the parties to arrive at the final destination of mutual satisfaction.

Business training seminars and instructional books teach the science of negotiation. For instance, anyone can learn the basic tools for establishing proper competency, tone, and culture during a negotiation. In contrast, the art of negotiation can only be developed through experience, sensitivity, and a humanistic approach.

Remember that negotiation is a relational process. The negotiation journey does not just deal with spreadsheets and financial reports, but addressing the heart-felt desires of both the buyer and seller. Often unspoken, emotional, health, and family issues are an integral part of the sale and/or purchase.

Communication and emotional factors are the backdrop to the tone of the negotiation. Although they are not the forerunners of the process, they are significant enough to define the outcome of a negotiation. Therefore, these issues cannot be dismissed as too warm-and-fuzzy

and not business-minded. Likewise, as the buyer, seller or intermediary, your integrity, credibility, and character are important stabilizing foundations in the negotiation process.

The negotiation process is comprised of a meaningful sequence of events. Like the layers of a pyramid, each phase is designed to support and secure the next layer of construction. However, all stages of negotiation work to arrive at the pinnacle of the negotiation process—satisfaction and success. The chart below outlines the negotiation milestones as it relates to the business sale or merger process:

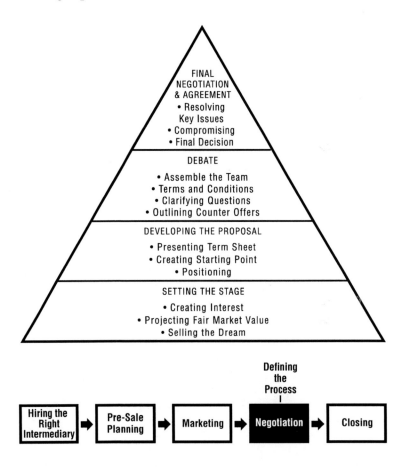

Chapter 13
Setting the Stage

The first stage in constructing a successful negotiation is to lay the foundation. Setting the stage creates the arena and parameters in which negotiations occur. The three main steps to setting the stage are as follows:

1. **Creating Interest**
2. **Selling the Dream**
3. **Determining Fair Market Value**

1. Creating Interest: The first behind-the-scenes step involves the seller establishing a goal or desired outcome. Every successful endeavor begins with a goal in mind. As discussed in the pre-sale planning section, defining the goals of the seller is key to having a satisfactory result. At this stage in the sale process, it is important to further define your personal objectives as they specifically relate to each potential buyer.

Everyone has needs, so it important to first identify them up front. The buyer may be in need of diversifying an existing business to obtain synergistic value and efficiency. Meanwhile, the seller may have health issues that are

prompting him to sell his business and retire. Needs are as diverse as the parties involved.

In addition, more than one need may serve to catalyze the negotiation process. It is human nature to avoid change until the pain of a current situation becomes unacceptable. The threshold of unacceptability varies among individuals. When that threshold is met, the need for change becomes so significant, that an individual is willing to make a change, explore a solution, and consider the negotiation process.

Uncovering these needs requires thoughtful insight and open communication. During initial meetings it helps to reflect on challenges each party is currently facing, stresses that could potentially be eliminated, and the amount of pleasure each party would feel if they could solve one of their most important issues.

From a buyer's perspective the plot may unfold in the following manner:

1. The need: A desire for greater financial success
2. The need fulfillment: Acquisition or merger of a profitable entity
3. Attainment of goal: Purchase a profitable entity

From the seller's perspective, the plot may unfold in the following manner:

1. The need: A desire for a financial security and retirement

2. The need fulfillment: Sale of their profitable entity
3. Attainment of goal: Sale of their profitable entity

Remember that sales and negotiation involve human beings, including their psychology, emotions, and complexities. We all have an innate, intuitive sense about others. At times, our "sixth sense" can aid us tremendously. Other times, there may be misjudgments that can severely affect relationships and negotiations. Be conservative at playing amateur psychologist and remember—a little knowledge can be a dangerous thing.

Case in Point: A buyer falsely assessed the needs of the seller. The seller had conveyed that he needed to sell his company due to serious health issues. The seller did not have any family members that could act as business successors; hence, the seller wished to transfer the company to new ownership as soon as possible. The buyer mistakenly assumed that the seller was desperate, and that he would save the day while cashing in on the seller's predicament.

The buyer made an initial offer that was 40% below the seller's proposed sales price. The seller was offended and felt that the buyer was being greedy and attempting to take advantage of the seller's predicament. The initial offer was so far off the mark that the seller did not respond. A second buyer submitted a more reasonable offer, and before the first buyer could resubmit, the deal had been sealed with the second buyer. Misjudgment and miscalculation caused the first buyer to sabotage and lose a great opportunity.

2. Selling the Dream: Fulfilling the Need: Once both parties begin to reveal their emotional needs, the human element begins to surface. Listening and learning is essential to a successful negotiation process. At this point, emotions fuel and are integrated into a dream or built into a plan. Therefore, the ability to identify and fulfill emotional needs is an integral part of any transaction.

An experienced intermediary knows how to merge the desires of both the seller and the buyer and showcase how the transaction will successfully fulfill both needs. The advisor can point out the synergies between the two parties. Once a buyer can see that purchasing a business from the seller will not just get him a business, but will fulfill his need, then the negotiation can truly begin to come together.

3. Determining Fair Market Value: To keep the negotiation on track, it is important for both parties to establish realistic guidelines in regards to fair market value. Perceived value varies among individuals, including sellers and buyers. A seller may determine their organization's value not only upon standard measurements, but also upon emotions and intangibles, such as the initial investment of sacrifice, sweat and heartache.

The pre-sale planning section discussed several factors which affect the value of a business. If a seller has successfully followed many of the guidelines in the pre-sales planning section, he or she will have a good idea of the fair market value of their company. By getting a fair and accurate picture of the business value, an owner will be less

likely to undergo the roller coaster ride of emotions during negotiation.

For example, any start-up business owner will have battle scars from the trauma and tribulation of birthing and nurturing a business from infancy to infamy. The blood, sweat and tears element of a business is intangible, yet not unreal, and is often a factor in the seller's calculation of value. If an owner consults with an intermediary, understands the current market conditions of the industry, and establishes a well thought out goal in regards to sales price, he or she will have a much healthier expectation once receiving proposals.

Chapter 14
Developing the Proposal

Once a buyer's interest evolves into desire, the seller has achieved the first milestone in the negotiation phase. At this juncture the buyer is ready to submit his first proposal. The first proposal is usually rendered in a less formal proposal document, known as a "**term sheet**" or by a more inclusive document known as a "**letter of intent**".

Not unlike the act of courtship, the **term sheet** represents a possibility. It is a distant proposal that requires the agreement of both parties before the relationship can be further developed. The term sheet may be binding or non-binding, depending on intent and wording.

The term sheet addresses most of the major issues and qualifications with less specificity, while revealing the starting point and basic structure of a proposed transaction. It will set the underlying tone of the negotiation from a posturing standpoint. It also allows the parties to determine whether there is enough common ground to move further into the negotiation process.

Prior to entering formal negotiations, the selling party requests a buyer to submit a term sheet after an adequate amount of information has been transferred to the buyer. This frequently occurs in a competitive

115

environment when there are multiple buyers or unusual circumstances.

For instance, after a successful marketing campaign, the seller may have more interested prospective purchasers than time would allow. After exploration with each candidate, the seller may request a term sheet from each of the buyers in order to weed out those that are not in the anticipated target range or value. This would help identify the top 10 or 20 candidates.

By defining the buyer's intent through a term sheet, the seller can quantify the merits of the offer without investing a significant amount of time. This is especially helpful when there is much disparity between the parties. Term sheets are useful tools when used properly, but at times, may be too indistinct to carry the intended impact.

Keeping in the mind the characteristics, purpose and limitations of the term sheet, it is important to thoroughly understand the intent of this initial negotiation tool. By using a seasoned negotiation team, a seller will avoid pitfalls and misunderstandings.

Like the term sheet, the **letter of intent** may be binding or non-binding depending on intent and wording. As compared to term sheets, the letter of intent may have the appearance of a more definitive agreement. Most letters of intent outline and define terms and conditions such as: contingencies, timing of key events, due diligence, allocation, training, and covenants.

In addition, the letter of intent may contain a "no-shop" clause that disallows the seller from marketing the entity to a third party for a specified time. This allows time to pass for the removal of certain contingencies. Since these clauses could cost the seller opportunities, most sellers require a substantial, non-refundable deposit from the buyer.

Letters of intent address and specify most of the major details of a deal and reveal the starting point and structure of a proposed transaction. Like the term sheet, the letter of intent establishes the underlying tone of the negotiation and allows the parties to determine whether there is sufficient common ground to develop the negotiation process.

Letters of intent may be intentionally non-binding, with intentional elements omitted, in order to gain leverage or advantage in the negotiation process. Many sellers and buyers have been forced into unfavorable situations by what appeared to be informational, non-binding negotiations. It is *very* important to understand the intent of the instrument used and ensure that proper wording accomplishes the intention of the author.

In contrast to a term sheet, the letter of intent may provoke more insight and thought, bringing some of the larger underlying issues to the forefront. A well thought out letter of intent is the cornerstone of a smooth transaction. Furthermore, when transitioning to the final purchase agreement, the letter of intent does not require as much additional participation and further negotiation.

Letters of intent include the following elements:

- Due diligence (usually a 20 day period)
- Timeframes and deadlines
- Liquidation clause
- Sign-off period
- Final allocation

Letters of intent are more detailed with regard to legal and financial issues and require greater control and input by the intermediary. Establish a solid letter of intent early in the negotiation process so you can easily incorporate agreed upon terms and conditions and details.

At this point, emotions are calm. Tap into this opportune time and control the moves with logic. Things should be well thought out and calculated, not based on 'feeling'. In fact, the only emotion that usually exists at this juncture is excitement on the part of the buyer.

Since this stage is a critical step to a successful negotiation, it is important to understand how to jumpstart the process. There are two ways the seller can begin the proposal; with an initial price offering or without an initial price offering.

If the seller enters the negotiation with an initial price proposal, he sets the tone, establishes the starting point, and "goes first". If the seller enters the market without an initial price proposal, the buyer must "go first" and establish the starting point through an initial price proposal. This can be an advantage to the seller, because it allows him to understand the buyer's positioning and what

is of value to the buyer. Knowledge is wealth, and in the following example, it is worth $400,000:

Case in Point: A specialized distribution company valued at approximately $2 million (on the high side) entered the market without an asking price. The buyer offered $2.2 million and eventually the transaction closed at a selling price of $2.4 million (20% in excess of seller's valuation). In this case the marketplace perceived value differed from the buyer's perceived value. If the seller had entered the market with an initial proposal of $2 million, he would have closed the door on a higher price and most likely received less than anticipated.

Whether the initial price proposal arises from the buyer or seller, it reveals the perspective of the originator. Akin to a courtship, the buyer and seller are constantly assessing the other and evaluating whether there is a chance of a future agreement. This courtship phase allows any parties to terminate early in the negotiation process, without having invested significant amounts of time and money. On the other hand, if the parties agree to move forward, they enter the next phase of negotiation, the debate.

Chapter 15
Debate

If the seller accepts the term sheet or letter of intent, the parties enter into the arena of debate - the center tier of the negotiation process. This juncture may be one of the most critical stages of the journey. The debate becomes the moment of truth where interest transitions into assessment and dictates whether the negotiation process will undergo metamorphosis or dismantling.

Until this point the negotiation has been fairly straightforward. All parties have been attempting to optimize their position. Communication has been generally non-binding and flexible, while both parties have invested minimal time, resources, and emotions. Throughout the negotiation, the intermediary acts as a third party buffer, privy to confidential information and perspectives of the seller and possibly the buyer. Now, the intermediary acts as choreographer, synchronizing the dance between the buyer, seller, and third party professionals. In order to avoid missteps and ensure a smooth and cooperative relationship, the intermediary is critical.

In the debate phase, there is a refinement of the communication process. The intermediary establishes the buyer and seller's true intentions towards a path of convergence. Realize that the debate process is not merely

about price, but also terms and conditions, which are powerful negotiating tools that can make or break a deal.

The opening statement of the debate typically consists of a binding opening proposal, thereby setting the tone for future dialogue. In fact, the opening bid is the primary factor in determining whether a seller will go forward. A seller needs to determine if the buyer's opening proposal (including price and major terms and conditions) passes the reasonability test. Once both parties have decided it is mutually beneficial to proceed, the debate involves the following steps:

1. Assembling the Team
2. Establishing Terms and Conditions
3. Clarifying Questions
4. Outlining Counter Offers

1. Assembling the Team: At this stage, the buyer and seller each bring forward their team of representatives. All team members should have experience in mergers and acquisitions. In addition, it is appropriate and expected that the buyer and seller inquire about the experience and number of transactions possible team members have had in their career.

For instance, do not hire counsel merely because he has been a friend, family accountant, or attorney. Team members who are novices in the mergers and acquisition area can increase the cost of negotiations, construct the transaction so that it is non-bankable, form delays, and unwittingly create tax liabilities due to lack of vision.

Case in Point: A buyer selected his family attorney as legal counsel. Although he was a good attorney, he had little experience in mergers and acquisitions and the value of the proposed transaction. For reasons that remain unknown, his counsel took up to two months to respond to the seller's counsel concerns and up to one month for any legal response. Because of these delays, the legal negotiation between attorneys continued for close to one year with no finality or conclusion. These delays ultimately cost the buyer the entire transaction; not to mention time and money invested in the negotiation process.

Additionally, there should be a clear chain of command within the team. It is generally beneficial for the intermediary to serve as the captain of the ship. One important note is that the seller and buyer should have separate representative intermediaries and team members. Additionally, all parties should insist on a cooperative spirit within their team.

Cooperation among the team members and an understanding of the leadership role of the intermediary is critical to maintain momentum in the negotiation process. Be wary of experts with strong personalities who overstep their appropriate roles. This results in power struggles and disagreements among team members with each competing for control. A seasoned intermediary will keep the negotiation process intact by maintaining momentum, establishing protocol, and taking the lead.

Conversely, some buyers and sellers believe that

they can reach an agreement without the presence of an intermediary at this point. There is a misconception that a business sale or acquisition is no more challenging or complicated than negotiating the purchase of a vehicle, for instance. The truth is a business merger or acquisition is much more challenging and complicated than a simple sales negotiation. Some obvious differences include:

- Monetary value is greater
- Consequences are higher
- Legal structures must be binding
- Financing of an often intangible entity is more complex
- Emotional elements need to be tethered

Case in Point: The sole shareholder of a manufacturing and distribution company was ready to retire. He wanted to sell the company to key management without financing the deal. The key management had little of their own capital along with five different personalities and functions. Four of the five were married, which meant nine individuals had to be satisfied.

Prior to engaging an intermediary, the seller had tried unsuccessfully to put together an agreement. He had abandoned the management buyout idea and was ready to sell the company on the open market. With the experience and commitment of the intermediary, the seller was able to achieve his objective of selling the company to his key management. The acquisition team was not only able to bring all the parties together, but the seller also received the

majority of the purchase price in cash through arrangement of third party financing.

The presence of an intermediary helps avoid common pitfalls, such as personality conflicts, pride, naivete, unrealistic expectations, technical and legal ignorance as well as inexperience with financing issues. A seasoned and competent intermediary is an essential element in the negotiation process.

Case in Point: A competitor took away market share and revenues from a logistics service company. The owner of the logistics company had other businesses and wished to sell his logistics company to concentrate on his other endeavors. Due to the competitive environment, strong entrepreneurial personalities, and ill will between the company and its main competitor, it would have been almost impossible for the logistics companies to see eye to eye enough to reach a deal.

The logistics company decided to hire an intermediary with broad experience in many types of companies and situations. As a result, the intermediary successfully negotiated the areas of conflict and created an agreement with the competitor. Meanwhile, the intermediary insulated the seller from the time-consuming process and emotional roller coaster ride of negotiation. The seller was able to stay focused on day-to-day operations, keeping the value of the company high during the protracted negotiation process. As a result, the seller received a premium price, which gave him significant growth capital for his other endeavors.

2. Establishing Terms and Conditions: Once the buyer and seller establish an experienced team of advisors, the debate turns to terms and conditions. Terms and conditions can range from the traditional to the creative. Regardless of the type or tone of the items, the practice of compromise is indispensable.

Examples of terms and conditions:

- The amount of post-sale business interest that remains for the seller
- The annual rate of return
- The amount of post-sale risk for the seller
- The degree of financing carried by the seller
- The tax structure (i.e. asset vs. stock sale)
- Health insurance or other group plans available to the seller after close of transaction
- Use of business perks and privileges (i.e. season tickets to sporting events, company limousine, etc.)
- Maintaining current employees and continuity that the seller has spent his life building

Some creative terms and conditions may be perceived as unpredictable or odd. Nevertheless, all should be seriously considered. Always remember that the term or condition may be what determines the outcome of a negotiation and deserves significant attention. What are you willing to accept or reject? Can you yield or compromise without future regret? You can influence the direction of the negotiation process by creating and sculpting terms and conditions.

In addition, don't be afraid to think outside the box or be creative. Every negotiation process is complex and may require provocative solutions and ideas. For instance, if the seller has an entity that harvests apples, but the buyer desires a business that makes applesauce, develop solutions. Perhaps the buyer can acquire the apple harvesting entity to add synergism to an existing apple processing business? Make a deal out of what is not there and introduce new elements to fulfill the needs of the other party. The most successful deals have innovative ingredients and elements.

Case in Point: A manufacturing company that was once part of a larger entity had recently gone through a management buyout and was ridden with an overwhelming amount of short-term debt. The company had developed a number of new opportunities. However, being under capitalized, the ownership was backed into a corner and felt that the only option was to sell. Since it was sold from a larger corporation, the newly acquired company had no verifiable sales and profit history other than current internal financials. In addition, the business had over-committed itself and timing was a concern.

After an intermediary reviewed the situation, he contacted a previous client who owned a number of companies. One of the client's companies was in the same industry. As a result, the intermediary successfully merged the current ownership with the new acquirer by utilizing a stock redemption, stock purchase, and reallocation package. The intermediary arranged for a new placement of financing which gave the company enough working capital to manage

and sustain growth. The seller became the buyer and the company has since become a stronger force in its vertical market.

3. Clarifying Questions: During the clarification phase of debate, wisdom and experience shine. A seasoned intermediary is aware of the unanswered questions that may emerge and has the posture to answer them with confidence. Keep an open mind and be prepared to discuss any details and issues. Artful posturing during this phase involves the following rules of thumb.

Keep quiet - Game playing can deter negotiations, yet it is also not advantageous to "give too much away" in the form of information and motives. By keeping quiet you decrease self-vulnerability, minimize opponent power, listen, and learn.

Be aware of body language - Not all communication is verbal. In fact, experts estimate that up to 93% of communication is non-verbal. Here are some unique ways to create an advantage when a price or concession is proposed that require significant compromise: flinch, demonstrate shock, let out an exasperated sigh, or do not answer. These non-verbal tactics are not always representative of how you really feel. In other words, they may be non-verbal communication techniques for which the buyer or seller has been coached so they may not accurately reflect their thoughts. Game playing is not encouraged during the negotiation process, but strategy and wisdom are, which comes from knowledge, listening and learning.

Avoid inaccurate assumptions - Assumptions can

influence behavior, but what if those assumptions are inaccurate? Remember the warning about amateur psychologists.

Avoid cost breakdowns - Assigning a monetary value to principle assets can potentially serve as points of contention between the buyer and seller. For example, perceived asset value may differ from fair market value. Don't create unnecessary obstacles in the negotiation process.

Make concessions - For the negotiation process to be successful, all parties must have the same goal: to create satisfaction. Arriving at gratification is an art; one must give a little, yet leave room to negotiate further. For instance, if the buyer opens with a proposal that is too high and demanding, he has placed himself in a position where there is little room to maneuver. Likewise, if the seller opens with a proposed price that is too low, he has placed himself position where there is little room to maneuver.

Be stingy but balanced - Despite the importance of compromise and concession, don't give away the farm! Stay balanced in your negotiations. Being stingy will help you stay in control, maintain your position, and save face.

The seller has a greater ability to maneuver if multiple offers and buyers are present. This should be the goal of the seller as well as the intermediary. Because of the great influence multiple buyers present, a buyer should be aware of competition and his negotiating environment.

Furthermore, the seller typically has the advantage in controlling the negotiation process, as it is typically the

seller who is granting concessions. If the seller masks his true feelings and sports the "poker face", he is less likely to be approached for an excessive number of concessions. On the other hand, avoid excessive stonewalling. If there is a lack of cooperation among the parties, you run the risk that the buyer will "walk".

The negotiation process is not a monologue of what one party demands, but rather a dialogue among parties. If one party yields to a request, then they should expect something in return. Furthermore, don't get ridiculous when requesting concessions. The expression "it can't hurt to ask" does not apply here. It can hurt to ask if you alienate your opposition and discredit your maturity as a negotiator.

During this stage of clarification, the role of the intermediary reaches a higher level. Because this negotiation phase can be regarded as "the heat of the battle", the intermediary becomes the emotional buffer between parties. The buyer and seller can become weary during the debate phase. As a result, the intermediary must keep deadlines in mind and all issues in perspective, such as making minor concessions for minor issues.

4. Outlining Counter Offers: Debate will inevitably consist of counter offers involving price, terms, and conditions. The counter offering phase can be brief (one counter offer), or tedious (10 or more counter offers). In this intense phase, parties can grow weary, so it is increasingly important for the intermediary to maintain momentum in the process. The "out of sight, out of mind" mentality is a

dangerous consequence in the world of business sales and acquisitions. The "strike while the iron is hot" mentality is more productive. You have arrived at the central milestone in the negotiation process; keep the momentum going through meaningful open dialogue and continuous communication.

Two essential ingredients to remember at this phase are listen and learn. Learn how to fulfill the needs of the parties by truly listening. Both buyer and seller must be educated about the relevant needs, expectations, compromises, and concessions of the other party. Compromise only on those terms and conditions that matter. It is not productive to concede to matters that are of no value to the other party. Understanding that value is not the same for everyone. Never negotiate, concede, or propose a term or condition until you know what it is worth to you and the other party. Remember that when the needs of all involved are satisfied (price, terms *and* conditions), the transaction is likely to close.

Chapter 16
Final Negotiation & Agreement

During the final negotiation phase, price, terms and conditions are agreed upon. Key issues are reviewed, formalized, and accepted. Parties are near the closing process, without actually resolving the transaction yet.

Key issues are settled in this phase. A rule of thumb to use here is "keep all things in perspective". Don't stumble on the minute or be ignorant to how all things work together. Shortsightedness and tunnel vision can ruin an opportunity. Consider the following scenario:

Case in Point: A buyer and seller were negotiating the acquisition of a successful business with a monthly net profit of $50,000. They were $100,000 apart on price. At this phase, all other terms and conditions had been agreed upon, but the disparity in acquisition price stalled the transaction. The buyer, firm on his offer, pulled out of the deal and did not purchase another entity until 12 months later. During his yearlong shopping period, he lost $600,000 ($50,000 x 12 months) worth of net income he could have enjoyed if he had been willing to come up $100,000 to meet the seller's asking price. What was the true cost of the buyer's missed opportunity?

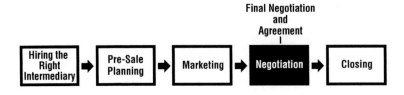

Many transactions get within 95% of closure, yet they fail to close because of unwillingness to compromise. This resistance to compromise may arise from egos, offense, and bad feelings created during the negotiation process. Often, tunnel vision emerges and the big picture gets lost. The win-win situation is dampened behind excessive focus upon pettiness. At this point, all parties have made a significant time and financial commitment participating in the negotiation process. Don't let shortsightedness be a stumbling block.

Amidst discussions, it is important to maintain the momentum of the negotiation process. A previously agreed upon deadline and time restraint helps ensure that the process does not stall. In addition, circumstantial, economic, and/or self-imposed pressure can help to fuel the momentum of the negotiation process. For instance, the buyer may feel pressure to merge with or acquire an entity, particularly if it will provide synergistic value to an existing company. On the other hand, the seller may feel pressure to arrive at a sales agreement if there is an urgent need for cash or health issues exist.

Throughout the negotiation process, all parties should think proactively and structure the transaction around the question: Is it executable? Are all legal issues allowed? Is financing a reasonable possibility? Once these final questions have been resolved, a seller is ready to begin the final step of the closing process. The next section will discuss how to structure transactions, the tax ramifications, due diligence, and finally close the deal.

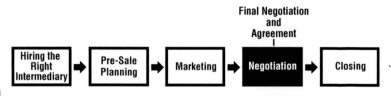

Section V

Closing

Chapter 17
Structuring the Transaction

Many transactions never come to a final closing due to the lack of preparation regarding the closing process. In this section we will discuss the importance of proper planning during this final stage.

The purchase or sale of a business entity is usually a very complex transaction. Is the deal classified as a "merger" or "acquisition"? Will this be a stock sale or an asset purchase? How do the various types of entities (corporations, S-corporations, LLCs, partnerships, individuals, trusts) affect the deal? In addition to these factors, there are federal tax laws, contract laws, and regulatory laws which are often complex. This section will highlight the importance of structuring the transaction, tax considerations, due diligence, and closing the transaction.

Roles of Professional Advisors

Many key people and professionals become involved in the process of selling a company. Some of these individuals may include management, the board of directors, stockholders, investment bankers,

intermediaries, bankers, brokers, accountants, appraisers, lawyers, management consultants, and regulators. This section will focus on the importance of the professional advisor, and in particular, the advisors associated with due diligence and the closing process.

Typically, management has a very large role in any transaction because they essentially run the company. In smaller companies, management is usually the owner or stockholder and has more of a role to play than non-owner managers. During the course of a transaction, management will not always have the technical expertise to handle all of the decisions that will be made. However, management provides direction, usually retains professionals, interfaces with the board of directors (if applicable) or owners, and eventually plans the integration of the deal.

If a company has a board of directors, the board is responsible for establishing the overall direction of the company and looking out for the stockholders' interest. In closely held companies, the owners and or key management are most likely the stockholders and will fill the role of the board of directors.

Intermediaries, brokers, and investment bankers are involved with marketing, deal structuring, negotiating, and closing a transaction. Additionally, investment bankers and intermediaries are often involved in obtaining financing to complete a transaction.

Attorneys assist in negotiations, perform legal due diligence, draft contracts and various other

agreements, and render legal opinions.

CPAs and accountants perform due diligence, tax planning, business valuations, audits as well as prepare prospective financial statements and issue comfort letters.

The closing process usually involves negotiations on how the transaction will be structured, the type of transaction, form of consideration, and tax planning considerations. During this final stage of a deal, having a team of competent professional advisors on your side is invaluable.

Types of Transactions - Mergers and Acquisitions

During negotiations, the parties establish a purchase price and a general idea of the exchanged assets. The major objective of structuring a transaction is the ability to transfer the expected value of the deal to the seller while operating within buyer constraints. The type of structure depends on the law, the tax code, and the creativity of the professionals involved in the deal. Typically, the professional intermediary, the attorney, and the accountant are the key players in structuring a transaction.

It is important that the intermediary work very closely with the other professionals to assure that the basic terms of the deal are in accordance with what was basically agreed upon during the negotiation process. The intermediary will often be the quarterback during this stage.

Before successfully structuring a transaction, a seller must understand the different types of deals. Basically there are two types of transactions: **mergers** and **acquisitions**. Mergers are essentially marriages of companies, where the parties become co-owners in a single remaining entity. The type of transaction depends on the desired outcome of the parties involved.

In an acquisition, the buyer acquires the business from the seller. This can be accomplished by purchasing the individual assets ("asset purchase") of a company or by purchasing the outstanding common stock ("stock purchase") of the company. The majority of transactions in the middle market are acquisition-type deals. The following section will discuss the different types of transactions and outline the general benefits and pitfalls of each.

Mergers

Mergers can be very complex and are rarely used in middle-market transactions. Mergers, which are sometimes referred to as business combinations, are essentially two companies which desire to operate as one company. Generally, there is an acquiring business entity attempting to absorb another business entity by financing the deal with the acquiring company's common stock.

There are different kinds of mergers, such as forward mergers, reverse mergers, subsidiary mergers, and triangular mergers. In a forward merger, the target

company is merged into the acquiring company, and the target stockholders receive the acquiring company's stock. In a reverse merger, the acquiring company is merged into the target company, and the acquiring company stockholders receive the target company's stock. In a subsidiary merger, the acquiring company incorporates a subsidiary company into its existing structure. All of these structures are very complex in nature and have different legal, accounting, and tax consequences.

Mergers and acquisitions usually take place because the merging of two companies usually results in synergistic benefits to the remaining merged company as a whole. A myriad of efficiencies and cost savings translate into a more profitable and valuable company.

Potential benefits of a merger include:

- Little or no cash up front
- Tax-free transaction, which allows the deferral of capital and ordinary gains taxes
- Operating efficiencies
- Cost savings
- Avoidance of bulk sale notification expenses and various legal obligations

Potential problems of a merger include:

- The buyer does not realize major post-closing tax benefits

- The seller is exposed to a value risk in the new stock issue
- The seller usually wants to receive some cash
- Valuation issues move forward
- The buyer assumes liabilities
- Controlling stockholders are potentially diluted

Acquisition - Asset Purchase

The acquisition of a company can be executed in two ways. The buyer can either purchase the individual assets or the ownership interest of the company. If the company is a corporation, the ownership interest is the common stock of the company. Buyers usually desire asset purchases, while sellers generally prefer the sale of their common stock interest in the company.

An asset purchase can also be complex in nature. In an asset purchase, the buyer is purchasing individual tangible assets of the company and in some cases, intangible assets such as goodwill, competition covenants, patents, etc. Additionally, the buyer will assume some of the target company liabilities on specific assets.

Careful planning and due diligence should be performed in cases where there are potential environmental liabilities or where regulatory authorities may be able to pursue damages against a new owner. These events could force the new owner to seek relief from damages against the seller. Other potential issues which require planning and due diligence include

product liability, union contracts, bulk sales statutes, and bankruptcy statutes regarding conveyance of property.

Asset Purchase - Buyer's Perspective

Most buyers prefer the purchase of a company's assets because the buyer is insulated from any known or unknown business liabilities. The buyer only inherits liabilities such as loans that encumber certain assets, like equipment or real estate. Generally, loans, lease agreements and other related contracts have to be renegotiated because they are not automatically transferable to the buyer. Favorable tax consequences exist for the buyer depending on the classes of assets that are being purchased.

Buyers prefer an asset purchase in the following situations:

- The buyer only wishes to purchase certain assets of the company, not all
- The buyer wishes to avoid the purchase of certain assets of the company
- The buyer wishes to terminate unfavorable collective bargaining agreements
- The buyer wishes to avoid costly underfunded employee benefit plans
- The buyer does not have sufficient financing to purchase the entire company
- The buyer seeks to avoid potential unknown liabilities

- The buyer seeks to avoid the assumption of current liabilities
- The buyer seeks favorable tax treatment of the acquisition

Conversely, buyers do not wish to engage in an asset purchase when:

- The asset purchase triggers unfavorable tax consequences to the buyer
- The buyer is not able to avoid certain liabilities
- Certain key intangible assets may not be assignable
- An asset purchase deal may trigger the maturity of debt
- There is a risk of fraudulent conveyance
- It is difficult to comply with bulk sales statutes
- There are lengthy cost and time delays to complete the transaction

In most cases, the buyer will prefer an asset purchase because of the basis step-up, which produces favorable tax treatment, the avoidance of known and unknown liabilities, and the avoidance of the purchase or assumption of non-desirable assets.

Asset Purchase - Seller's Perspective

In most cases the seller of a company would prefer the sale of the ownership interest (common stock

if a corporation). In an asset sale the seller is generally stuck with unfavorable tax consequences and may be saddled with certain undesirable assets and liabilities. However, there are instances where good tax planning can produce opportunities for a seller to favor an asset purchase.

These favorable seller opportunities include:

- The company being sold is an asset for tax purposes, so the asset sale produces the same results as a stock sale
- Current tax attributes, such as net operating losses and capital loss carryforwards, may help alleviate the corporate level gains from an asset sale
- Tax consequences might be favorable, depending on the current tax basis of individual assets versus the stock basis of the individual stockholders
- Proceeds from the sale of the assets will be reinvested into new business ventures, eliminating tax at the liquidation level

Careful planning by a skilled, experienced intermediary, in conjunction with the legal and accounting professionals, can lead to the development of an asset deal that will serve both parties' interests, thus, getting this type of deal to close.

145

Acquisition - Stock Purchase

Provided that the selling company is a corporation, the alternative to purchasing the assets of a company is through the purchase of the outstanding common stock of the company. The buyer essentially purchases all of the outstanding common stock of the target company for a specified purchase price. The buyer replaces the seller as owner and becomes the new controlling stockholder.

Stock Purchase - Buyer's Perspective

When a corporation's stock is bought, the buyer has acquired all of the assets as well as known and unknown liabilities of the company. If the company has only a few stockholders, a stock purchase is generally less time consuming since the complexities of transferring assets do not apply. However, a corporation with many stockholders can create additional expense, time delays, and complications in a stock transaction.

The benefits of a stock purchase to the buyer include:

- Favorable tax attributes, such as net operating losses and capital loss carryforwards
- The continued use of certain accounting methods that might otherwise not be available
- Continued use of the name of the company

- The continued use of leases and contractual rights
- Assumption of a favorable debt structure
- The assumption of favorable collective bargaining agreements
- The assumption of favorable insurance rates and credit ratings
- Lower transaction costs
- Significant time savings to close the transaction
- Rules regarding the allocation of purchase price are avoided

The problems with a stock purchase to the buyer include:

- Assumption of all actual and contingent liabilities
- Detailed due diligence would be required to gain comfort
- Dissenting stockholders may prevent 100% ownership of the company
- Loss of the tax basis step-up of assets

Stock Purchase - Seller's Perspective

The seller in a stock transaction will generally realize favorable tax benefits resulting from long-term capital gains treatment at the stockholder level. Generally, no corporate-level taxes arise from the

transaction. The stock transaction eliminates the second-tier tax, which can arise when sale proceeds are distributed from the seller's corporation to its stockholders. The stock transaction also provides for easy liquidation of the investment to cash.

The benefits of a stock purchase to the seller include:

- All liabilities are transferred to the buyer
- Generally, no corporate-level tax
- Eliminates the second-tier tax on liquidation
- Eliminates the cost of liquidation
- Uses tax-free reorganization
- Transaction can be completed in a more timely manner

Generally speaking, the seller will favor a stock purchase primarily due to the tax benefits realized in the transaction as well as the ease of exiting the company. Careful planning by the mergers and acquisitions professional, in conjunction with legal and accounting professionals, can lead to the development of a stock deal that will serve both parties' interests, thus, getting this type of deal to closing.

Forms of Consideration

It is obvious that structuring a merger or acquisition requires the decision to structure a

particular transaction as an asset or a stock purchase. In addition, it is important that the transaction structure have a desirable form of consideration for both the buyer and seller. Consideration is generally defined as the form of payment that will be made to consummate the transaction. The different types of consideration include cash, common stock, preferred stock, installment notes, options, warrants, convertible securities, and earnouts or contingent payments.

Cash is the most desirable consideration because there are no valuation issues and it is perfectly liquid. Cash is straightforward and it creates no complexities in structuring the transaction. Conversely, the use of common stock generally creates valuation issues. When the buyer cannot finance the entire transaction, preferred stock and seller-financed notes are commonly used.

The buyer and seller settle on contingent payouts (earnouts) when they cannot agree on the value of the company. Based on predefined goals that are related to revenues, operating income, or net income, contingent payouts are made to the seller in future periods. The contingency is usually specified as a percentage of the contingent objective. The earnout provisions typically settle the valuation difference perceived between the buyer and the seller.

When structuring an earnout, the purchase agreement must be very specific about:

- Accounting methods to be used
- Limitations on the payout
- Whether the earnout is based on cumulative or annual performance
- The measurement period
- The income stream to be used in the calculation
- Provisions for auditing the calculations
- The date the earnout is payable
- Impact of extraordinary items

The factors stated above relate specifically to the form of the earnout provision and how the transaction will ultimately be structured.

The following additional factors have significant impact with regard to structuring the transaction and include:

- Will the seller retain an interest in the company?
- Will there be a lease agreement with the seller?
- Indemnification and contingency clauses
- Management consulting agreements
- Non-compete agreements
- Employment contracts
- Payout terms
- Interest rate
- Covenants

- Security agreements
- Default provisions
- Responsibility for closing costs

The form of consideration is a vital part of structuring the transaction. A thorough understanding of the type of transaction necessary, in conjunction with the transaction structure, provides an opportunity for both the buyer and seller to achieve their desired results.

Chapter 18
Tax Considerations of Transaction Types

The tax consequences of structuring an asset purchase transaction versus a stock purchase transaction are completely different. The asset purchase transaction requires the allocation of the purchase price over the different classes of asset that are being purchased. The stock purchase transaction has no such requirement.

Asset Purchase - Tax Considerations for the Buyer

Once the purchase price has been determined, the general tax consequences to the buyer are determined by how the transaction is ultimately structured. In accordance with Internal Revenue Code (IRC) Sec. 1060, the purchase price must be allocated based on one set of fair market value considerations. The allocation must be included in the transaction documents and also reported to the Internal Revenue Service in the tax year of the transaction. Form 8594 is used for reporting the transaction on the buyer and seller tax returns. It is very important that there are no

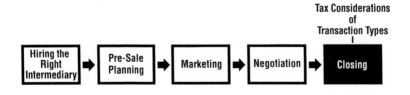

inconsistencies in the tax filings.

Temp. Reg. 1.1060-1T(c)(2) separates trade or business assets into seven classes:

I. Cash and equivalents
II. Actively traded personal property defined in IRC 1092 (marketable securities) and certificate of deposits
III. Accounts receivable, mortgages and credit card receivables in the ordinary course of business
IV. Stock in trade or other property that would ordinarily be included as inventory
V. All assets not included in I - IV above
VI. IRC Sec 197 intangibles except goodwill
VII. Goodwill

At this point in the transaction, there is a significant amount of planning which can be done with regard to tax and accounting issues. In reviewing the seven items in Temp. Reg. 1.1060-1T(c)(2), it is obvious that through planning and negotiation, the allocation of the purchase price can have a significant impact on the desired outcome of the transaction. Once the asset purchase transaction is closed, the buyer has purchased a group of assets which now have a new holding period. The buyer must then make various tax elections for the treatment of depreciation and amortization. As we have previously discussed, all other tax attributes remain with the seller in an asset purchase transaction.

Asset Purchase - Tax Considerations for the Seller

The sale of trade or business assets in an asset purchase transaction results in taxable gains and losses to the seller. Gain or loss will be determined on each individual class of assets sold. Again, it is important to stress the importance of pre-planning with regard to structuring the allocation of purchase price in the transaction.

After the determination of gain or loss has been made, the advisors must decide if the gain or loss will be capital gain/loss or an ordinary gain/loss. Capital gains currently enjoy a maximum federal tax rate of 20% while ordinary gains are included in income and taxed at an individual's effective tax rate. Capital losses are limited to $3,000 after netting against capital gains. Ordinary losses are fully deductible in the year of loss.

Because of the many different forms of consideration, the seller must understand the consequences of accepting a cash deal, seller-installment notes, or an earnout provision. Allocation of the forms of consideration must also be pre-planned so that the seller achieves a desirable outcome.

Before settling on a final purchase price and consideration, the following tax planning pointers are recommended for sellers in an asset purchase transaction:

- Consider any debt that must be paid off at closing
- Consider the form of consideration (payment)

- Consider the amount of cash desirable at closing
- Consider the tax consequences

Stock Purchase - Tax Considerations

There are three ways to accomplish the sale of a business other than the sale of the individual assets.

1. The stockholders of a corporation can dispose of their common interests through a taxable stock sale. A taxable stock sale results in the target corporation remaining in existence with all tax attributes of the corporation remaining with the corporation. The individual stockholders recognize gain on the sale of their individual interests. Generally, there is no corporate level tax unless an IRC Sec. 338 election applies.

2. The stockholders of a corporation can dispose of their common interests in a tax- free reorganization. A tax-free reorganization generally results in no gain or loss to the selling stockholders.

3. The stockholders of a corporation can dispose of their stock through a forward cash merger. For tax purposes, this type of transaction treats the target company as selling its assets to an acquiring company followed by a liquidation.

The focus of this section is to expand on the first example, a taxable stock sale transaction. The different tax considerations will be compared to a direct asset sale.

Generally, when a corporation owns appreciated

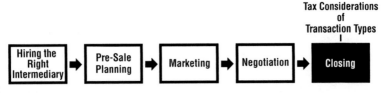

assets, a tax problem exists for one of the two parties involved. If a stock sale is executed, the buyer has deferred tax liabilities moving forward. If an asset sale is executed, the seller will owe depreciation recapture and capital gains taxes.

Case in Point: Jeff is the only stockholder. Jeff has a basis in his stock of $100, while ABC corporation's only depreciable asset has a tax basis of $400. ABC corporation has a net operating loss carryforward of $300.

ABC Corporation	FMV
Assets	$ 2,000
Equity	$ 2,000

If Jeff sells his stock to Heidi for $2,000, Jeff will recognize a capital gain of $1,900 of which he will pay $380 in Federal income taxes (assuming a 20% capital gains rate). This will leave Jeff $1,620 on the transaction net after taxes. The stock sale will not affect the carrying basis of the individual assets or liabilities and the buyer will retain all of the tax attributes. Jeff will be happy because he can now walk away from ABC corporation because it will still be in existence. Jeff also will avoid the cost and additional taxation of a corporate liquidation.

If Jeff sells the assets to Heidi for $2,000, ABC corporation will recognize a taxable gain of $1,600, of which $300 can be offset by the net operating loss. The

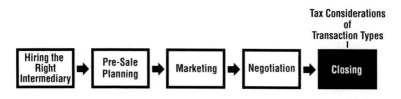

corporate tax liability will be $195 (assuming a 15% tax rate). If Jeff then liquidates the corporation and pays the tax liability, $1,805 will be distributed to Jeff as a liquidating distribution of his stock. Jeff will recognize a capital gain of $1,705 and pay capital gains taxes of $341. The asset sale utilizes the corporation's tax attributes, and the buyer will have a new basis in the assets that she has purchased. Jeff is not happy because he received less under this asset sale transaction.

The preceding illustration is a simple way of showing the tax implications to the buyer and seller based on the transaction as an asset sale or a stock sale. Careful planning and knowledge of the various tax implications of each type of transaction is crucial. The benefit to the buyer is usually a problem for the seller and visa versa.

Planning at this stage of the transaction should be creative enough so that the desired outcome for the buyer is also a positive for the seller. This desired effect cannot always be accomplished. Thus, the importance of having a good team working with the buyer and seller cannot be understated.

All too often, the buyer's tax advisor will attempt to kill the deal because of the structure of the deal. Or the seller's tax advisor will attempt to alter the deal because the amount allocated to the non-competition agreement is too high. The intermediary understands the needs of both, is experienced at negotiating differences, and can coordinate with the tax professionals to best achieve the desired outcome for all parties.

Tax Considerations of Transaction Types

New Tax Developments

The Financial Accounting Standards Board (FASB) issued two new accounting and reporting standards during 2001. Statement no. 141, Accounting for Business Combinations, and Statement no. 142, Accounting for Goodwill and Intangible Assets, represent major rule changes affecting mergers and acquisitions.

Statement no. 141 - Accounting for Business Combinations

A company may no longer use the pooling-of-interests method of accounting for a business combination as of June 30, 2001. The new standard requires that companies use the purchase method of accounting for all business combinations consummated subsequent to June 30, 2001.

Statement no. 141 essentially supercedes APB Opinion no. 16, which outlined the basic accounting rules that must be used for business combinations prior to June 30, 2001. APB no. 16 allowed a business combination to be accounted for either as a pooling-of-interest (pooling method) or a purchase (purchase method) transaction.

The pooling method was required if certain criteria were met, otherwise the purchase method was to be used. When the pooling method was used to account for a business combination, the balance sheets of the

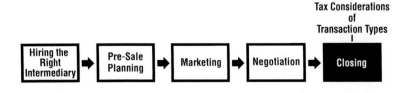

merging companies were essentially merged or added together. The premium paid over the book value of the merged company was not required to be recorded. The resulting balance sheet of the merged companies did not reflect the fair value of the assets purchased in the deal. Consequently, the new merged company did not have to write-off amortization expenses relating to the premium paid by the acquirer. Therefore, the net income of the company may be overstated using this method of business combination.

The purchase method requires that the assets purchased be recorded at fair value. The purchase method further recognized the premium paid for the assets of a company by the recording of goodwill. Goodwill is the difference between what a company paid for an acquisition and the book value of the net assets of the acquired company. Goodwill is an amortizable intangible asset. The resulting balance sheet under this method would indicate the fair value paid by the acquirer. Amortization expense would reduce earnings over time to the extent that a premium was paid for the company.

It is obvious to see that the application of either of the methods will result in potentially significant differences in financial statement results. Moreover, the differences between the pooling and purchase method could affect competition in markets for mergers and acquisitions. The basic approach of Statement no. 141 is that all business combinations are acquisitions and should be accounted for in the same way based on the

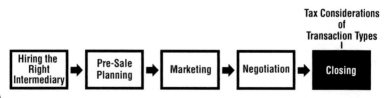

values exchanged.

Statement no. 141 - Illustration:

ABC Company has the following balance sheet:

Current Assets	$ 100,000
Property and Equipment	900,000
Total Assets	$ 1,000,000
Liabilities	400,000
Common Stock	500,000
Retained Earnings	100,000
	$ 1,000,000

DEF Company has the following balance sheet:

Current Assets	$ 1,000,000
Property and Equipment	200,000
Total Assets	$ 1,200,000
Common Stock	1,000,000
Retained Earnings	200,000
	$ 1,200,000

DEF Company agrees to exchange 100,000 shares of its common stock valued at $1,200,000 for all of the common stock outstanding of ABC Company.

The following illustrates the business combination using the purchase method:

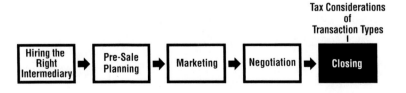

Current Assets	$ 1,100,000
Property and Equipment	1,100,000
Goodwill	600,000
Total Assets	$ 2,800,000
Liabilities	400,000
Paid-in-capital	1,200,000
Common Stock	1,200,000
	$ 2,800,000

The following illustrates the transaction using the pooling method:

Current Assets	$ 1,100,000
Property and Equipment	1,100,000
Total Assets	$ 2,200,000
Liabilities	400,000
Common Stock	1,200,000
Paid-in-Capital	300,000
Retained Earnings	300,000
	$ 2,200,000

The preceding illustration is to show, in a very simplistic way, how the recording of assets, liabilities, and equity differ using both the pooling and purchase methods. Essentially the purchase method records the excess of fair value over the net value of assets, which in this example is $600,000. The pooling method merely combines the balance sheets without recording the fair value of the deal.

Statement no. 142 - Accounting for Goodwill and Intangible Assets

The elimination of the pooling method described previously will now force all companies to account for a business combination under the purchase method. However, Statement no. 142, which supercedes APB Opinion No, 17, has substantially changed the purchase accounting method. More than likely, this standard has been issued to make the purchase method more attractive to companies in conjunction with removing the pooling method as an option.

The traditional purchase method required a company to record goodwill. Again, goodwill is an intangible asset representing the difference between what was paid for an asset and the book value of the acquired assets. Additionally, periodic amortization charges were required to be recorded against the earnings of a company that held goodwill on its balance sheet over a period not to exceed forty years. Amortization charges had become a drag on the earning power of a company and potentially affected the underlying value of the company.

Statement no. 142 now allows a company to make acquisitions without having to take amortization charges against earnings. Goodwill does not have to be reduced by amortization charges. The reasoning is that intangible assets are considered an economic resource and represent the underlying synergies of a business combination. The value of such does not necessarily erode over time. As such, these synergies now need to be measured as of the

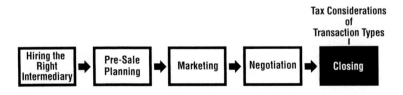

balance sheet date to determine the synergistic value to the company. In lieu of amortization charges, an impairment charge will be used to reduce the value of goodwill subsequent to an analysis of the asset. This is to determine whether there has been a change in the economic life or future synergies of the asset.

Tax standards and codes are subject to change. Regardless of the current state of tax consequences, a professional intermediary can effectively bridge the chasm between the best possible outcome for the buyer and best possible outcome for the seller.

Chapter 19
Due Diligence

So far, this section has highlighted the different types of transactions, how these transactions can be structured, and tax planning issues for the buyer and seller. Prior to developing a purchase agreement, it is vital to both the buyer and seller of a business that they fully understand these planning aspects.

The development of a purchase agreement begins informally during the negotiation process. Generally, the buyer has specific information regarding the target company such as financial statements, tax returns, employees, customers, etc. As the negotiating process moves forward, the buyer and seller agree on price and terms and a letter of intent is drafted.

As discussed in section 4, the letter of intent is a document that indicates that both the buyer and seller are serious about executing a purchase agreement and consummating a deal. The letter of intent will effectively define the due diligence procedures and obligate the buyer and seller to carry out those procedures within a specified date. For purposes of this section, we will focus on the due diligence procedures that should be performed by the buyer and seller.

Due diligence is the process of conducting an investigation to determine the full implications of a proposed transaction. Once the parties have reached a formal agreement to allow the investigation, the due diligence process can begin. The scope of a due diligence program is determined by the following:

- The size of the target company
- The type of company
- The buyer's experience and knowledge of the company
- The type of proposed transaction
- The proposed form of consideration

There are several levels of due diligence which can be performed. They include financial due diligence, legal due diligence, and operational due diligence.

Financial and operational due diligence generally include:

- Identification of potential deal-breakers
- Verification of information and representations
- Obtaining more details regarding the transaction
- Obtaining vital information for structuring the deal

Legal due diligence generally includes:

- Verification of ownership aspects of the target
- Search for undisclosed liabilities

- Review of various pertinent legal documents
- Assisting in preparation of language and preparation of purchase documents

The due diligence process operates in various stages involving a variety of professional advisors. It is important that the letter of intent fully outline the various stages and provide timelines for completion of the due diligence process. Generally, the due diligence process is undertaken in a discreet way to prevent employees and outside parties from discovering the potential transaction. The seller must be cooperative during the process to assure that the buyer can complete due diligence in a timely fashion. The buyer, in turn, should avoid unnecessary procedures and disruption of the seller's business operation.

As the due diligence process begins, it is important to have one party responsible for overseeing the process so that it moves smoothly. Additionally, any problems that may arise can hopefully be resolved soon after they are discovered. Once again, the intermediary is the prime candidate to quarterback this very important process. The intermediary ultimately makes sure that the proper level of time is being devoted to each area of the due diligence process. Moreover, the intermediary is more suited to resolve any deal-breakers that may arise.

In most cases, the due diligence process requires the use of professional advisors such as accountants, lawyers, and other experts. The roles of these professionals will sometimes overlap, causing unnecessary costs and delays.

Once again, this problem can be avoided by using an intermediary to coordinate the other professionals through the process. The intermediary works with the buyer and the seller to resolve issues as they arise and keeps the process moving at a reasonable pace. It is important that this phase of the transaction move quickly and efficiently.

The following sections will discuss the objectives of due diligence from the buyer's perspective and the seller's perspective.

Due Diligence - Buyer's Perspective

From the buyer's perspective, the due diligence process assures the buyer that he gets what he is paying for. Additionally, the buyer must be confident that he is not paying too much for the target company.

The buyer's due diligence program is designed to gather information that assesses the value of the target company. The true condition of the seller's company ultimately determines its value to the buyer. This includes the general risks affecting the financial condition and operations of the target company. It also includes the future plans of the target company. Therefore, it is important to properly plan the due diligence investigation to achieve the proper results.

The buyer prepares a due diligence program that provides the following:

- Layout of the different procedures to be performed
- Assign responsibility for these procedures
- Set appropriate deadlines for completion of the various procedures
- Evaluate the findings and results of the procedures
- Resolve issues that have been uncovered

The following is an example of a fairly standard due diligence program from a buyer's perspective:

General Procedures

- Determine when the company was formed
- Determine the legal structure
- Determine equity owners
- Determine fully diluted effects of financial derivatives
- Names of the Board of Directors
- Determine the history of the current equity holders

Products and Services

- Determine the various types of products and services
- Determine the length of time of the various product lines
- Identify pricing procedures

- Identify product branding, patents, copyrights, and trademarks
- Identify expiration dates on the above items
- Identify licensing or franchising agreements
- Identify regulatory issues
- Identify warranty liability
- Identify new technology and research developments
- Identify strengths and weaknesses
- Obtain brochures
- Obtain product manuals
- Obtain major agreements
- Obtain applicable third party information

Competition

- Identify competition
- Identify market share statistics
- Identify competitive strengths and weaknesses
- Identify new technology that might be competitive
- Identify articles in trade journals on current trends

Sales and Marketing

- Develop an industry profile
- Identify general customer base
- Identify general market share
- Identify geographical sales breakdown

- Identify seasonal variations
- Identify sales backlog
- Identify marketing methods used
- Identify growth prospects
- Identify current customer base and repeat business
- Identify sales force
- Identify sales training programs

Purchasing and Production

- Identify major products
- Identify product components
- Identify major product component costs
- Identify custom specifications, if applicable
- Identify purchasing practices
- Identify terms of purchase
- Develop an overview of the production process
- Identify inventory methods
- Identify inventory costing methods
- Identify quality control practice

Facilities and Equipment

- Determine size of facility
- Determine type of construction
- Determine when built
- Identify any existing leases
- Obtain equipment lists and depreciation schedules

- Review age and condition of equipment
- Review repairs and maintenance expense
- Identify any appraisals
- Identify insured values
- Inquire and review expansion plans
- Review historical capital expenditures
- Inquire of any environmental problems
- Review production efficiency and capacity
- Obtain leases
- Obtain insurance policies
- Obtain appraisals

Management and Employees

- Identify key management personnel
- Identify board of directors
- Identify major stockholders
- Identify hiring process
- Identify management practices
- Identify key employee turnover
- Identify general employee turnover
- Identify compensation and fringe package
- Identify existing employee benefit or pension plans
- Identify collective bargaining agreements
- Identify compensation claims
- Obtain organizational charts
- Obtain employee handbooks
- Obtain key employment agreements

Financial Review

- Review financial statements
- Review cash flow
- Review monthly cash receipts and disbursements
- Identify key financial ratios
- Identify capital structure
- Identify accounting system
- Identify management information systems
- Identify general accounting practices
- Identify accounting policies
- Identify control process
- Identify banks and major creditors
- Identify off-balance sheet assets and liabilities
- Identify non-recurring items
- Obtain financial statements (minimum five years)
- Obtain tax returns (minimum five years)
- Obtain loan agreements
- Obtain accounts receivable aging
- Obtain accounts payable aging
- Obtain inventory details
- Obtain current business plans
- Obtain financial projections or forecasts

Other Key Elements

- Review intangible assets
- Review expiration dates for existing copyrights and patents

- Identify franchise agreements
- Execute a UCC filing search
- Review other publicly filed documents existing
- Compliance with bulk sales laws
- Determine liability for transaction and closing costs

Due Diligence - Seller's Perspective

The due diligence process is a significant process to the buyer. However, furnishing the due diligence documentation to a buyer presents considerable work for the seller. Once again, an intermediary is invaluable in this process. The intermediary does not allow the due diligence procedure to begin until he has received the letter of intent and draft copy of the purchase agreement from the buyer. This is important since the buyer and seller should not have any unresolved major terms before the due diligence process begins.

The intermediary, being familiar with the due diligence process, begins to gather relevant information from the very beginning of his engagement. Throughout all phases of the sale, the intermediary is working to clear any issues that could result in problems during due diligence. During the actual process, he can then act quickly to clear any issues that arise and threaten to derail the sale.

Aside from the considerable work to furnish documents for the buyer's due diligence, the seller does not have as detailed a process.

The seller's major concern is getting paid. If the proceeds are to be paid in total at closing or if part of the deal is structured as deferred payments, the seller is mainly interested in the buyers ability to pay. The intermediary has pre-qualified potential buyers before the negotiating process. However, the seller should apply due diligence procedures to make sure the buyer is capable of coming up with the proceeds to close the deal.

The seller should include the following procedures:

- Obtain buyer's financial statements to verify financial status
- Obtain a credit history on buyer
- Identify other buyer deals
- Review public records for legal issues concerning buyer
- Obtain bank references
- Obtain business and personal references
- Obtain representations from buyer regarding financial history

If the seller is providing financing, his or her due diligence procedures should also assess the buyer's ability to pay on the outstanding balance of the note. Depending upon the length of the time negotiated on the note and the outstanding balance, these procedures can be extensive.

The seller should include the following procedures:

- Obtain buyer's financial statements to verify financial status
- Obtain a credit history on the buyer
- Identify the source of funds for the downpayment
- Identify the source of funds for deferred payments
- Review public records for legal issues concerning the buyer
- Obtain bank references
- Obtain business and personal references
- Obtain representations from the buyer regarding financial history
- If other guarantees on the loan exist, perform similar procedures
- Evaluate existing collateral for the note
- Depending upon the results of the due diligence, demand additional collateral
- Consider the use of life insurance

Other Due Diligence Considerations

The seller should always be concerned about the buyer's business plan. The business plan outlines the buyer's strategy, existence of resources, and ongoing working capital of the business. Reviewing the business plan is a prudent due diligence procedure.

In addition, the seller should have a clear understanding as to which party is obligated on the various closing costs, such as transaction fees, broker, or intermediary fees. A thorough review of various sections of

the purchase agreement, such as a non-compete covenant, may require the use of professionals. The earnout provisions of an agreement may also require the use of an outside professional. Additionally, performance clauses with regard to financial ratios may exist in the agreement and require the use of outside professionals.

The due diligence process is extremely vital and should be addressed with care. A professional intermediary should have experience in all aspects of this process and can guide you down this potentially hazardous path.

Case in Point: A client engaged a merger and acquisition firm to perform a due diligence review of an acquisition target. The seller's books were in good order and the company appeared to be clean. The due diligence review included a comprehensive lien check which disclosed certain state tax liens that were never disclosed for unpaid taxes. The intermediary notified the client of the circumstances, and because of the nature of the liens, the deal never went to closing.

Had the seller engaged an intermediary sooner, the intermediary would have identified this particular stumbling block early in the process and worked with the owner to manage the issue.

Chapter 20
Closing Documents and Procedures

This chapter will discuss in detail the documents and procedures involved in closing the sale of a business. Although the focus is on papers and processes, it is extremely important to note that careful and skillful planning is required during the transition to avoid operational and organizational problems. Any number of conflicts can arise at this point of the closing process, such as key employees leaving, customers seeking alternative suppliers, and credit issues with existing vendors. These challenges could potentially reduce the underlying value of the seller's business.

Many of these issues could also become a problem for the acquiring business owner. Employees may fear that their jobs are in jeopardy, customers may be worried about existing services and contracts being fulfilled, and vendors and other creditors may be concerned about existing financial commitments. For a new owner, the most common problem during the closing process is the unknown.

The answer to the problem is communication.

Proper communication to employees, customers, vendors, and creditors go a long way to answer the many questions that are being asked. Alternately, lack of communication leads to rumors, which generally creates problems, such as those discussed in the preceding paragraph.

Generally, an internal memorandum to employees can prevent many rumors and answer many questions. In addition, direct or written communication to customers, vendors, and creditors usually keeps any external problems from beginning. To develop an integration plan, it is valuable to form a transition team comprised of representatives from both the seller's business and the acquiring business. The team should include department managers, as they are most intimate with the intricate details that will need to be dealt with as the process moves on.

The intermediary can also play an instrumental part in easing the tensions between the buyer and seller. The intermediary already has the basic knowledge of how both companies operate and he is able to bring management together quickly to develop an integration plan. The intermediary can also be an invaluable negotiator for any problems that may arise, so that they can quickly be resolved and the process can move forward.

An integration plan should be crafted so that it encompasses the broad functional areas that need to be combined or eliminated. The acquiring company already understands the business synergies that exist and the cost savings from combining or eliminating certain departments.

The transition plan should include a review of the following:

- Organizational controls and responsibilities
- The compatibility of financial reporting practices
- The compatibility of business information systems
- The compatibility of production practices
- Identifying opportunities to benefit purchasing capabilities
- Identifying opportunities to benefit marketing capabilities
- The compatibility of compensation and employee benefit plans
- Identifying redundant activities
- Identifying business synergies created by the deal

Closing Documents

The acquisition or purchase agreement is the definitive controlling document for the deal. The purchase agreement is essentially the road map for when and how the deal is to be completed. In addition, the purchase agreement outlines and explicitly defines the terms, obligations, and remedies of the deal. The purchase agreement is a legally binding document.

The buyer's attorney usually prepares the purchase agreement in draft form. All parties then review the draft and make modifications. When the negotiating process has been finalized, the basic terms and conditions of the deal are fully

detailed in the purchase agreement so that both parties are bound legally to complete the transaction.

The intermediary plays an important role during this process as a "go between". The intermediary solves many problems that arise during this process and is extremely valuable to both the buyer and seller in accomplishing a final purchase agreement.

Purchase agreements are generally in a standard format and consist of sections that relate to the following list where applicable. Generally, the purchase agreement contains the following sections:

- **Introduction**
- **Terms of the Deal**
- **Representation and Warranties of Buyer and Seller**
- **Pre-Closing Obligations**
- **Pre-Closing Conditions**
- **Post-Closing Obligations**
- **Miscellaneous Provisions**
- **Closing Procedures**

The **Introduction** section of the purchase agreement usually contains the names, addresses, and various background information regarding the buyer and seller.

The **Terms of the Deal** are fully defined in this section of the purchase agreement. A typical "terms"

section includes the following:

- Detail of the assets or stock to be sold
- The sales price
- Terms of payment
- Installment payment provisions, if applicable
- Applicable interest rate, if applicable
- Security for the installment note, if applicable
- Supplemental guarantees for the note, if applicable
- Contingent payout provisions

It is important that a detailed description of every asset (applicable to an asset purchase only) and the associated sales price has been identified in the purchase agreement to satisfy IRC Sec. 1060.

The **Representation and Warranties** section of the purchase agreement includes statements made by the buyer and seller that are considered factual. The seller may be asked to verify that the financial statements are true and correct as well as include all assets and liabilities that exist at the closing date. The seller may ask for representations from the buyer regarding certain abilities or other documentation that was used during negotiations. Warranties are guarantees that certain conditions exist. The buyer or seller may warrant that a certain license is valid and in good standing. The applicable representations and warranties are developed throughout the due diligence process and become formalized in the purchase agreement.

The **Pre-Closing Obligations** section of the purchase agreement generally defines the activities that the buyer and seller have undertaken during the period between the signing of the purchase agreement and the closing date. Pre-closing obligations can include anything from making records available for inspection to maintaining certain assets on the balance sheet. The importance of this section is that it clearly defines what the buyer and seller are obligated to do preceding the closing date.

The **Pre-Closing Conditions** section of the purchase agreement generally defines certain conditions that must be satisfied prior to or at the closing. These items can include gaining regulatory approvals, insurance coverage, and verification of certain pre-closing obligations.

The **Post-Closing Obligations** of the buyer and seller define the actions that are taken if the buyer or seller representations are inaccurate. The language included in this section of the purchase agreement can include the following:

- Obligatory payments based on specified financial activity
- Indemnification clauses including specified remedies
- Liquidating damages provisions
- Obligations relating to non-compete agreements
- Obligations relating to consulting or employment agreements

The **Miscellaneous Provisions** section of the purchase agreement generally covers the following:

- The state laws governing the purchase agreement
- Transaction fees
- Responsibility for transaction fees
- Arbitration procedures
- Circumstances by which the agreement will be in default
- Circumstances by which the agreement will terminate

The **Closing Procedures** section of the agreement defines the documents, property, and considerations that are used to complete the transaction. The following is a more detailed list of areas that are usually addressed in the purchase agreement:

- Identification of the buyer and seller
- General location of the buyer and seller
- General description of the assets and or liabilities that will be sold
- Details of major assets to be sold
- Buyer and seller warranties
- Description of seller business conduct to closing
- Details of conditions that precede the closing
- Termination provisions
- Mechanics of closing
- Indemnification provisions
- Covenants

- Responsibility for events subsequent to closing
- Bulk sale provisions
- Responsibility for transaction costs

In addition to the purchase agreement, there are other closing documents that are a part of the closing process. A brief description of some of the more common documents is as follows:

Settlement Statement: The settlement statement is a worksheet which outlines in detail the payments and expenses of the buyer and seller.

Promissory Note: If the deal is made on an installment basis, a promissory note is necessary. The note identifies the amount of the installment amount, the interest rate, a payment schedule, and usually defines the seller's rights in the event of late payments or a default.

Security Agreement: A security agreement accompanies a promissory note. The security agreement creates a public record to record the seller's interest in certain collateral which is named in the agreement.

Employment or Consulting Agreement: If the services of employees, owners or other consultants is a part of the deal, the details of the employment are provided in this agreement. The employment agreement outlines the amount of compensation to be paid, the types of service to be rendered, and the length of agreement time.

Transfer Documents: These include a "Deed" for real estate, or "Bill of Sale" for personal property. Any document describing the various types of property to be transferred from the seller to the buyer are considered transfer documents.

A well-planned closing is the desirable outcome sought by all parties involved. The closing process can be an extensive process depending upon the size of the deal and the amount of conditions which need to be satisfied. The majority of the work will be performed by attorneys and financial advisors. The intermediary still has the important role of keeping all parties on the same path and helping the seller get the very best deal.

Case in Point: A high-tech company decided to sell the business. Prior to engaging a mergers and acquisitions firm, the owner of the business had done various research regarding the value of the company and how to market the company. After a considerable amount of time had passed, the business owner received a very low offer and became very frustrated with the situation. After receiving no further offers, the business owner engaged a M&A firm.

The intermediary provided the necessary expertise in properly valuing the company and marketing that value to prospective buyers. Using an extensive network of marketing resources, the intermediary found a buyer within six months. Because of their expertise in determining business value, communicating value to prospects, understanding the marketplace, and negotiating terms, the client received

almost twice as much for his company compared to the first offer he had received!

The moral of the story, there is no substitute for a qualified intermediary to quarterback your deal to a close.